God Says Count
The Number
666!

666

I0107838

Why the Church <u>Can</u> Discover
the Identity of the Antichrist!

Charles K. Bassett

Positron 🌐
Books
Las Vegas, NV

To the Lord Jesus Christ,
God of Heaven and Earth

CONTENTS

* Note — This book assumes the reader has a good handle on the basics of Bible prophecy. *God Says Count the Number 666!* is not intended as an overview of the end times. It is meant to answer a particular question, namely, whether or not it's possible for the Church to learn the identity of the Antichrist before the Rapture. Nevertheless, I have tried to guide the reader (where appropriate) by clarifying how the possibility of discovering the Antichrist's identity dovetails with the overall prophetic tapestry.

For additional information on my eschatological framework, please see the Afterword and Appendix A, "Rules of Interpretation."

* * * The Challenge * * *

If you're reading these words, there's a pretty good chance you believe that no one today can know who the Antichrist is.

You believe that despite all the clues provided in Scripture, God has hidden that man from our eyes. You think that even though Jesus told us to decipher the book of Revelation, the 666 code is actually meant for post-Rapture saints. You are sure that Satan has been frantically grooming dozens of men for the last twenty centuries for the position of Antichrist, because not even the devil can know who the Antichrist is.

And above all, you know for a fact that when Paul says the Antichrist won't be "revealed" until after the Rapture, he means the Antichrist cannot be identified by anyone now.

So let me ask you something…

Does this make sense?

Paul: To the Frightened Thessalonians

Now we plead with you, brothers, about the coming of our Lord Jesus Christ at the Rapture. Please do not be shaken in mind, or troubled, neither by spirit, nor by word, nor by letter as from us, stating that the Tribulation has already started.

For the Tribulation will not start, until the Rapture comes first, and **that man of sin, the Antichrist, has been identified by someone who's been left behind**.

Don't you remember that when I was with you, I told you these things? And now you know what is holding the Antichrist back **until it is time for him to be identified**. Because even though the forces of Satan are hard at work behind the scenes, the One who now holds back the Antichrist will continue to hold him back, until that same One is taken out of the way at the Rapture.

And **then shall the Antichrist be identified**, whom the Lord shall consume with the spirit of his mouth, and shall destroy with the brightness of his coming.

So relax and stop worrying, dear brothers, because the Antichrist *will not be identified* until after the Rapture!

Paraphrase of 2 Thessalonians 2
according to most prophecy experts

...or does this?

Paul: To the Frightened Thessalonians

Now we plead with you, brothers, about the coming of our Lord Jesus Christ at the Rapture. Please do not be shaken in mind, or troubled, neither by spirit, nor by word, nor by letter as from us, stating that the Tribulation has already started.

For the Tribulation will not start, until the Rapture comes first, and **that man of sin, the Antichrist, is unleashed to begin his rampage**.

Don't you remember that when I was with you, I told you these things? And now you know what is holding the Antichrist back **until it is time for him to come to power**. Because even though the forces of Satan are hard at work behind the scenes, the One who now holds back the Antichrist will continue to hold him back, until that same One is taken out of the way at the Rapture.

And **then shall the Antichrist be let loose to begin his diabolical reign**, whom the Lord shall consume with the spirit of his mouth, and shall destroy with the brightness of his coming.

So relax and stop worrying, dear brothers, because the Antichrist won't be *unleashed to attack or persecute anyone* till after you're safely in heaven!

Paraphrase of 2 Thessalonians 2
according to Paul's stated desire to
comfort and calm the Thessalonians

* * * *

So…you still think Paul was saying that no one today can ID the Antichrist?

* * * *

Chapter 1

MISSION: IMPOSSIBLE?

THE VERDICT IS IN! The vast majority of pastors and prophecy experts are convinced it is absolutely impossible to identify the Antichrist today.

These good people are positively certain that any attempt to locate the Man of Sin before the Tribulation begins is doomed to failure. Even though many signs prove the Tribulation is near, the Antichrist himself cannot be discovered, they say. Indeed, from their point of view, it is wrong for the Church to even *think* about looking for him.

The 11th Commandment?

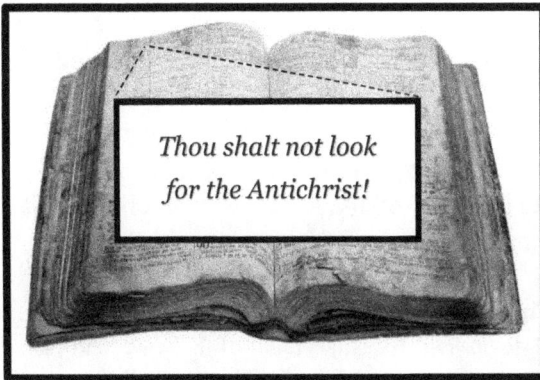

Thou shalt not look for the Antichrist!

I know that sounds like an exaggeration. But the fact is, most Christian leaders are *adamant* that no one today can discover the Antichrist. And several of the most popular prophecy teachers have made some very strong statements against those who attempt to locate the Beast:

Mark Hitchcock — Many have **grossly misused** gematria [letter-number substitution] to apply it to the names of modern leaders to see if they could be the Antichrist... All such **foolish speculation** should be avoided. The Antichrist will not be unveiled until the beginning of the tribulation period, or Day of the Lord.[1]

Dave Reagan — I never cease to be amazed at the **mental gymnastics** of those **obsessed** with identifying the Antichrist... since the Bible clearly teaches that we cannot know the identity of the Antichrist before the day of the Lord.[2]

Jeff Kinley — I don't think we can really know who the Antichrist is definitively right now... And if you do know who he is, then bad news: **You're in the tribulation**...[3]

I respect all of these men, and I esteem their knowledge of prophecy. But in view of their absolute certainty that no one can know who the Antichrist is, the obvious question is, what makes them so sure? How do they know *for a fact* the Antichrist won't be revealed until after the Rapture?

The answer is simple. It's because the apostle Paul apparently said so.

Paul's statement appears in Second Thessalonians. And, sure enough, verses 2:7-8 seem to support what our pastors and experts now teach. According to these verses, the Antichrist won't be "revealed" until the Church has been "taken out of the way" at the Rapture:

> **2 Thessalonians 2:7-8** (NKJV) — He who now restrains will do so until He is taken out of the way. And then the lawless one [the Antichrist] will be revealed...

---

[1] Mark Hitchcock, *Is the Antichrist Alive Today?* (Colorado Springs, CO: Multnomah Books, 2002) p. 67. [Boldface added.]

[2] David R. Reagan. "Prophetic Craziness: The Playground of the Sensationalists." The Lamplighter (Nov-Dec 2014) Vol. XXXV, No. 6. [Boldface added.]

[3] Billy Hallowell. "Who Really Is the Antichrist?" (CBN News: Faithwire) 3/4/2022. [Boldface added.]

Paul's statement is pretty straightforward. But for the sake of clarity, allow me to paraphrase: The presence of the Church is now restraining the Antichrist. The Man of Sin is being held back. Imbued with the power of the Holy Spirit, the Church is (effectively) preventing the Beast from rising and taking control of mankind. Consequently, the Church must be "taken out of the way" before the Antichrist can be "revealed." Only *after* the Rapture occurs and the Church is removed from this planet can the Beast be identified. And not a moment before.

In view of these facts, it's easy to understand why the vast majority of expositors insist that anyone who tries to identify the Antichrist today is on a "mission: impossible." According to them, Paul ended the debate nearly two thousand years ago when he said the Antichrist wouldn't be "revealed" until the Church was caught up to heaven.

What's more, the weight of precedent is on the expositors' side. For the last two thousand years not one so-called "Antichrist" has proven to be *the* Antichrist. Although many people have been accused of being the monster of Revelation—including Attila the Hun, Nero, Hitler, Mussolini, several popes, many European kings, and even a few U.S. presidents—not one of those accusations has ever proved true. Not one historical figure has ever turned out to be the Son of Perdition.

As a result, our pastors have endured nearly two thousand years of hearing people cry wolf, and they are (justifiably) tired of it. Given these precedents, and the passages that seem to support their position, who can blame our shepherds for thinking that looking for the Antichrist at the *present time* is a *waste of time?*

THE CATCH

Still there is a catch: The Bible never specifically declares the identity of the Antichrist off-limits to the Church. And some Christians think there's a reason for that:

I have an opinion. God tells Christians a lot of details about the man of sin that the world doesn't know about. **And I do believe the implication is that we, if we are perceptive, will be able to recognize the oncoming of the man of sin.** While the world does not suspect that he is the Antichrist, he will be obvious enough to perceptive Christians so we will be able to say, "There he is," and prepare for the almost immediate Rapture of the Church.[4]

Pastor David Breese

With due respect to the brethren who say otherwise, I must concur with Pastor Breese. I believe it is actually quite possible for the Church to identify the Antichrist just ahead of the Rapture. Why? Because in addition to Pastor Breese's insightful observation, the combined effect of at least eighteen statements in Scripture proves that it's not only *possible* for the Church to make this identification, but that God actually *wants* us to make it!

Let me repeat that: Despite the insistence by many well-meaning pastors and scholars that the Antichrist cannot be discovered till the Church is removed at the Rapture, a fair and impartial review of the relevant scriptures proves that God actually wants us to try to determine the identity of the Beast. Indeed, John the apostle actually commanded the Church to make the attempt:

> **Revelation 13:18** — Let him that hath understanding **count the number of the beast**: for it is the number of a man.

Remember, John addressed Revelation exclusively to the Church (Rev. 1:4, 22:16). Therefore, the Church is the entity that is supposed to decode verse 13:18 and "count the number of the Beast," not post-Rapture believers or anyone else.

---

4   Dave Breese, "Cyclone of Apocalypse," in *Forewarning: Approaching the Final Battle Between Heaven and Hell,* William T. James ed. (Eugene, Oregon: Harvest House, 1998), p. 322. [Boldface added.]

To be sure, I agree with the adage so often recited: *The Church is not waiting for the Antichrist, she is waiting for Jesus Christ.* Our focus must always be on the Lord and on the increase of his kingdom. Our job is to follow God's lead and to bring in the lost. But that doesn't mean we should pretend the prophecies about the Antichrist don't exist, or that it's somehow wrong to compare those prophecies against current world leaders.

The fact is, hundreds of godly men and women presently research the traits and future career of the Antichrist *specifically* to gauge how close our world is to the start of the Tribulation. And within the context of staying alert and determining our proximity to the Rapture, that kind of research is generally approved by most pastors. To my mind, the attempt to actually locate the "prince who is to come" (Dan. 9:26) would simply be an extension of that research and, consequently, should not be discouraged. In fact, the discovery of the Antichrist would be the most dramatic confirmation of prophecy since the rebirth of Israel in 1948 and would undoubtedly lead to the salvation of thousands of people who might otherwise miss the Rapture.

There is one caveat, however. While Scripture might permit and even *endorse* a search for the Antichrist, nothing in God's Word *guarantees* that discovery. That is to say, the identification of the Antichrist is conditional. God has left the possibility open, but it's up to us to do the actual investigating and to be on the lookout.

A NEW PARADIGM

The notion that it might be possible to identify the Antichrist today is a sharp break from conventional wisdom. Indeed, it's an entirely new paradigm. For years, the vast majority of preachers have taught that no one can learn the identity of the Beast until after the Rapture. And they've cautioned their congregations against looking for him.

Why is there so much resistance to identifying this monster? It's because, for years, hundreds of overly eager parishioners have spotted the "Antichrist" around every corner, and pastors are weary of having to calm their flocks.

Worse, these false "Antichrist sightings" have consistently brought reproach upon the Word of God, and they've caused a lot of disharmony within the Body of Christ. Consequently, when pastors advise against wild speculation and spurious accusations, it is *not* out of a desire to put anyone down. Instead, it is out of a genuine concern for God's people. Our pastors don't want to see anyone else distracted or harmed by this kind of sensationalism.

I therefore appreciate what it means to put forth a contrary viewpoint on such a sensitive topic. I understand what our leaders have been forced to endure, and I realize why they might resist the theme of this book. Nevertheless, I'm convinced that these good people, above all, want to know what the Bible actually says on this subject, even if that knowledge produces a major shift in the Church's thinking.

For that reason, it is with genuine respect that I offer the following arguments. I appreciate the pastors and scholars who've established the foundations of modern eschatology, and I value their priceless contribution to our understanding of Scripture. My desire is simply to add to that data by presenting a more complete and accurate assessment of the doctrine in question, namely, whether it's possible to discover the identity of the Man of Sin before the Church is taken to heaven. If I can at least start a positive conversation on this topic, I will count my efforts successful.

* * * *

Note – You will occasionally see a rule notation at the end of a sentence, such as "(Rule 2)." This indicates that the sentence or statement is based on one of my *Rules of Interpretation* (located in the Appendix), and the rule should be reviewed in order to grasp why that particular statement is valid. There are just ten rules and I believe you will find them to be both intriguing and enlightening.

Chapter 2

OVERVIEW

THIS ESSAY WILL DEMONSTRATE that it's not only possible for the Church to identify the Antichrist prior to the Rapture, but that God actually wants us to make the attempt.

I realize that's a pretty ambitious objective. But throughout the Bible, God promises to pull back the curtain on latter-day prophecy, the closer we get to the end. And nowhere does God exclude the identity of the Antichrist as part of that information "reveal."

Take a look at these five special statements about end-time prophecy and ask yourself: Do these statements make it more likely the identity of the Antichrist will be revealed today, or less?

1. **Jeremiah 23:20** – The anger of the Lord will not turn back until He has executed and performed the thoughts of His heart. In the latter days <u>you will understand it perfectly</u>.

2. **Jeremiah 33:3** – Call to me, and <u>I will answer you, and show you great and mighty things</u>, which you do not know.

3. **Daniel 12:9-10** – The words are closed up and sealed till the time of the end... none of the wicked shall understand, but <u>the wise shall understand</u>.

4. **Amos 3:7** – Surely the Lord does nothing, unless <u>He reveals His secret to His servants</u> the prophets.

5. **John 16:13** – He [the Holy Spirit] will guide you into all truth ...and He will tell you things to come.

The theme isn't hard to detect. If we call to the Lord and ask him about things to come, he will answer and show us *great* and *mighty* things. Why? Because *he reveals his secrets* to his *servants the prophets* until they understand such things *perfectly*. And that means, in the run-up to the Tribulation, it is *more likely* the Antichrist will be revealed because God has promised to send greater and greater insight, the closer we get to the end. And that insight is almost certainly going to include the identity of the Antichrist.

How can I be so sure of that possibility? Three reasons. First, because *nothing* in Scripture rules out the chance that the identity of the Antichrist might be revealed today. Second, because God *always* uses detailed prophecies to help his people escape judgment. And third, because Scripture actually *commands* the Church to try to determine the Antichrist's identity.

Does all of that sound hard to believe? Maybe. But the concepts I'm about to show you will prove every statement above. And I'm confident that if you examine the evidence for yourself, you'll find the analysis to be quite convincing, if not downright inspiring!

Indeed, it is difficult to imagine a more powerful fulfillment of prophecy—one that could actually help thousands of people to avoid the Tribulation entirely—than the confirmed existence of the Antichrist!

Let us therefore begin this exciting discussion by reviewing the overall outline. I've grouped our discussion into three easy sections:

- **Section I** contains seven arguments (1-7) which explain why *the knowledge of the Antichrist's identity is not off-limits to the Church.*

- **Section II** includes three arguments (8-10) which prove that *God uses detailed prophecy to help people escape judgment.*

- **Section III** consists of eight arguments (11-18) which demonstrate that *the Church is actually expected to make a bona fide effort to determine the Antichrist's identity.*

To be sure, no man or woman can know who the Antichrist is until that monster actually enters our world and is born in some dark corner of the planet. But aside from this limitation, not only is the Church permitted to research the matter, she can actually expect an answer *provided* she is diligent and seeks God in prayer.

Remember: God has said that those with "wisdom" should count the number of the Beast (Rev. 13:18). So perhaps we, as the Church, should pray for that "wisdom." [5]

In the meantime, let's begin by imitating the renowned Bereans and start searching the Scriptures to see whether these things are so.

---

[5] Solving the identity of the Antichrist depends on our willingness to study the prophecies and to pray for the "wisdom" needed to solve them (Rev. 13:18). It also depends on God's discretion to provide that wisdom. The revelation of the Antichrist's identity is therefore *conditional*. It requires both parties to make a conscious decision to act.

Sadly, one case where a conditional revelation did *not* result in the desired outcome occurred when the Jews rejected their Messiah in 32 A.D., forcing God to put the Kingdom on-hold for two thousand years. Had the Jews studied the prophecies and accepted the signs that Jesus had given to prove his identity, they would've been ushered into their time of rest immediately. The prophecies at Daniel 9:26-27 allow for either of these two paths because the fate of the Jews was *conditioned* on whether they would—or would not—accept their Messiah.

Likewise, I believe the discovery of the Antichrist's identity is conditional—it depends on God's willingness to provide the "wisdom" needed to spot the Antichrist. But it also depends on our willingness to research the matter and to be on the lookout.

Chapter 3

MAIN ARGUMENTS

SECTION I – *SCRIPTURE DOES NOT PROHIBIT THE CHURCH FROM RESEARCHING OR LEARNING THE IDENTITY OF THE ANTICHRIST*

THE FOLLOWING SEVEN ARGUMENTS demonstrate that despite what many expositors teach, nothing in God's Word prohibits the Church from researching or learning the name of the Beast.

 # 1. "Revealed" means *empowered* — not *identified*.

Let's begin this study by addressing the biggest elephant in the room, namely, Second Thessalonians 2:7-8:

> For the mystery of iniquity doth already work: only he who now letteth will let, until he [the Holy Spirit/Church] be taken out of the way [at the Rapture]. And **then shall that Wicked** [the Antichrist] **be revealed**.

Second Thessalonians 2:8 is considered to be the ultimate proof of today's anti-discovery doctrine. **This one sentence is supposedly what prevents the Church from learning the identity of the Beast.** Whenever a parishioner asks who the Antichrist might be, he (or she) can be sure that these words will eventually be cited to politely end the discussion.

The rebuke goes something like this:

> *Paul has said that the Antichrist will not be "revealed" until the Church is "taken out of the way." And up until now, every attempt to name the Antichrist has failed. Therefore, as far as God is concerned, the Antichrist cannot be identified at the present time. And it is patently foolish to keep looking for him!*

In short, the case is closed! The discussion has ended! That is the conventional wisdom espoused by most pastors and scholars today. The matter is not up for debate or discussion because the Antichrist will not be "revealed" until after the Rapture. So don't even look for him. Paul has already settled the matter!

Our pastors and scholars are good men of God and they have earned their positions through years of hard study and tested experience. We should always love and respect them. However, there is a huge problem with the argument above—one that ultimately affects the Church—and it needs to be addressed: The word "revealed" in Second Thessalonians does not mean to be *identified*. It means to be *unleashed and empowered*.

And because that is true (a fact we will prove in the next few pages), anyone who relies on Second Thessalonians to dissuade people from locating the Antichrist is posting a roadblock where none should exist. God never said, "Do not look for the Antichrist," in Second Thessalonians, or anywhere else.

In truth, Second Thessalonians was not written to dissuade people from locating the Antichrist. It was written to mark the sequence of end-time events, namely: the removal of the Church at the Rapture (first), followed by the empowerment of the Antichrist (second). That's all the passage was meant to convey. *Church safely removed, then Antichrist unleashed and enthroned.* Period. And the evidence for this is so overwhelming, it is almost impossible to deny.

That evidence includes:

- The meaning of the word "revealed" as used in the KJV

- Cause-and-effect

- The purpose of Paul's letter

- A stunning contradiction

Let us therefore start this section by taking a look at each of these concepts one-by-one. Let us consider them carefully and see whether the word "revealed" (in this passage) means to be *identified* or to be *empowered*. That is the critical task because **knowing what Paul meant by the word "revealed" is the key to this entire discussion**.

KJV Meaning of *Revealed* — The King James Version of the Bible is a priceless translation of the Greek and Hebrew manuscripts. Scholars have used this version for centuries to help them communicate the truth of God's Word. But several of the terms employed by the editors in 1611 A.D. (when the KJV was produced) have acquired completely new meanings and nuances. For example, *to let* used to mean *to hold back*. Today it means *to allow*. To be *careful* used to mean to be *anxious*. Today it means to be *cautious*.

Consequently, to establish the correct meaning of "revealed" in Second Thessalonians—i.e., the meaning that was intended by Paul —we need to see how that word is used in the New Testament, and then see how it's used in the context of Paul's letter. If we do that, I believe we'll discover that "revealed" simply means to be *unleashed and come to power*. It does not mean to be *identified*.

Take Romans 1:18, for starters. Here, Paul writes to the church about the Second Coming of Christ, and says:

> **Romans 1:18** — For the wrath of God is **revealed** from heaven against all ungodliness and unrighteousness of men, who hold the truth in unrighteousness.

Clearly, the word "revealed" in this context does not mean that God's wrath is going to be *identified* from heaven. It means that God's wrath is going to be *unleashed* from heaven. It is going to be *unleashed* and *let loose* against sinners. That is the meaning demanded by the context.

Again, in the First letter of Peter, where the apostle encourages the church to look to the future and to Christ's return, he says:

> **1 Peter 4:13** — But rejoice, inasmuch as ye are partakers of Christ's sufferings; that, when his glory shall be **revealed**, ye may be glad also with exceeding joy.

Clearly, Peter does not mean that Christ's glory is suddenly going to be *identified* when he comes in his kingdom. He means that Christ's glory is going to be *unleashed* when he returns. It is going to *reach its full power and extent* at that time. The context leaves no other option.

Again, in the Gospel of Luke:

> **Luke 17:28-30** — But the same day that Lot went out of Sodom it rained fire and brimstone from heaven, and destroyed them all. Even thus shall it be in the day when the Son of man is **revealed.**

Clearly, Luke is not saying that God's judgment will fall when Jesus is *identified* on earth, but when Jesus *comes to power* on earth.

So how is the word "revealed" used in Second Thessalonians? Well, in the very first chapter, it is used to say that Jesus is going to be *unleashed* and *take vengeance* on his enemies when he returns—not that he's going to be identified!

> **2 Thessalonians 1:7-8** — And to you who are troubled rest with us, when the Lord Jesus shall be **revealed** [unleashed] from heaven with his mighty angels, in flaming fire **taking vengeance** on them that know not God, and that obey not the gospel of our Lord Jesus Christ.

Pretty clear, isn't it? So why would Paul change that usage just a few sentences later? The answer is, he wouldn't and he didn't! Instead, he used it the exact same way:

Verses 2:3-4

For [the Tribulation] shall not come except ... **that man of sin be** *unleashed and take power*...

— NOT —

For [the Tribulation] shall not come except ... **that man of sin be** *identified as the Antichrist*...

Verses 2:7-9

[O]nly he who now letteth [holds back the Antichrist] will let [will continue to do so], until he be taken out of the way. And **then shall that Wicked be** *unleashed and take power*, whom the Lord shall consume with the spirit of his mouth, and shall destroy with the brightness of his coming.

— NOT —

[O]nly he who now letteth [holds back the Antichrist] will let [will continue to do so], until he be taken out of the way. And **then shall that Wicked be** *identified*, whom the Lord shall consume with the spirit of his mouth, and shall destroy with the brightness of his coming.

Remember, Paul was trying to calm the Thessalonians in the wake of a false rumor which said the Tribulation had already started (v. 2:1-3). Paul calmed the brethren by simply reminding them of what he had taught on a prior occasion, namely, that the Tribulation could not begin until: a) the rapture had taken place (a.k.a., the "*apostasia*" or the "departure"), and b) the Holy Spirit had stepped back to allow the Antichrist to come to power. Neither of those events had yet occurred, so the Thessalonians had nothing to worry about! The Antichrist *would not be unleashed* until after the church was safely in heaven. (See "The Purpose of Paul's Letter" on page 27.)

The discovery of the Antichrist's *identity*, on the other hand, had no bearing on the safety of the Thessalonians and was therefore not under discussion. It was completely irrelevant.

Moreover, there is not one instance in the New Testament (outside of this dispute) where the word "reveal" might mean *to uncover the secret identity of a certain person.* Not one!

And that is precisely why the Antichrist's "reveal" in Second Thessalonians *does not* lead to him being *identified* as Satan's emissary. Instead, it leads to his being *unleashed and empowered.* He is suddenly permitted to "oppose God," "sit in the temple," and "exalt himself" above the Almighty. That is what being "revealed" means in this context. [6]

* * * *

So, here is the takeaway: Despite what the experts have said, the phrase, "then shall that wicked be revealed," cannot mean *then shall that Antichrist be identified.* It has to mean *then shall the Antichrist be unleashed to take power.* Once the Church has been taken from the earth, then the Antichrist can be *let loose and begin his rampage.* The context of Second Thessalonians permits no other interpretation.[7] And that means Paul's letter does not prevent anyone from locating or identifying the Antichrist at this time. If this wasn't true, then Paul would be saying the Antichrist can't do the "working of Satan," or "oppose God," or "sit in the temple," or "exalt himself," until he has been *identified*, which makes absolutely no sense. And God's Word always makes sense.

---

[6]   This doesn't necessarily mean the Antichrist *will* be identified today, only that he *might* be. The doctrine of imminence negates any scenario in which some event *must* precede the Rapture; therefore, I do not claim the Church *will* identify the Antichrist today, only that it's *possible.* My paraphrase of 2 Thessalonians 2 in Appendix C should help clarify this.

[7]   Some might try to evade the demands of the context by claiming that "revealed" means *both* to be "identified" and to "come to power" at the same time — a clever move. But for that to be true, the word "identified" must *first* fit the context *all by itself.* It must be able to *stand alone.* Yet as we saw in *The Challenge* section, it can't. So pairing the two definitions in order to gain legitimacy for the one ("identified") is simply a dodge. It bypasses the required logic.

Cause and Effect — If you doubt this is the correct way to read these verses, the same conclusion can be reached by examining the cause-and-effect structure of Paul's statements. Take a look at verses 2:6 and 2:7. Both of these verses clearly state that the Holy Spirit (through the presence of the Church) is causing the Man of Sin to be *withheld* and *restrained*. They do not say the Holy Spirit is causing that monster to be *hidden* or *concealed:*

> **2 Thessalonians 2:6** – And now ye know what **with-holdeth** [restrains the Antichrist] that he might be **revealed** [unleashed] in his time.

> **2 Thessalonians 2:7** (NIV) – [B]ut the one who now **holds it back** [holds back the Antichrist] will continue to do so till he is **taken out of the way**.

The Restrainer is **causing** the Antichrist to be *restrained and held back*. He is not causing the Beast to be hidden or concealed. Thus, when it is time for the Antichrist to rise, and the Restrainer is "taken out of the way," the **effect** cannot be that the Antichrist will suddenly become identifiable as the Man of Sin, but that he will suddenly be *unrestrained* and *let go*. He will be *unleashed* to take his throne (v. 2:4). He will no longer be held back. Instead, he will be allowed to *come forth* so that he may launch his wars and embark on his rampage (Rev. 6:3). Once the restraint is removed, the Antichrist will be *free to rule* — not *free to be identified*.

Cause and effect.

The Purpose of Paul's Letter — During our investigation into Second Thessalonians and whether the Church can learn the identity of the Beast, we must always keep in mind that Paul's stated purpose in writing this letter was to calm the brethren by answering a specific question they had raised: *Are we now in the midst of the Tribulation or not? Did we somehow miss the Rapture?* That's all the church wanted to know:

27

2 Thessalonians 2:1-2 – Now we beseech you, brethren...
That ye be not soon **shaken in mind,** or be **troubled**...as
that the day of Christ [the Tribulation] is at hand.

The Thessalonians were "shaken" and "troubled" because someone had told them they had missed the Rapture and were now in the Tribulation (i.e., the "day of Christ" was "at hand.") Paul therefore responded to this concern by reminding the church that before the Antichrist could *be unleashed* (be "revealed"), and the "day of Christ" could begin, the believers had to be taken to heaven by Jesus. They had to be raptured before anything else could take place. The Thessalonians therefore had nothing to worry about. Jesus would remove them to glory before the Beast *was unleashed* and *given the power* to ravage the nations.

On the other hand, if Paul was saying the Antichrist could not be *identified* until after the Rapture, then his attempt at calming the Thessalonians would have fallen flat. After all, how would the inability of the Church to identify the Antichrist prove to the Thessalonians they were safe from that monster and not being persecuted by him already?

Indeed, a careful review of Paul's letter proves that no one had asked the apostle, *Who is the Antichrist?* or, *When will we know who he is?* And that is why Paul left those topics completely untouched. He never discussed the identity of the Beast—nor did he say it was pointless to look for him—because no one in Thessalonica had raised either issue.

All the Thessalonians wanted to know was whether or not they had entered the Tribulation. Paul told them they had not, *because the Antichrist had not yet come to power*. And whether the Antichrist would be identified prior to the Rapture—or after—had no bearing on when the Tribulation itself would begin.

Consequently, Second Thessalonians does *not* say it is impossible to identify the Antichrist today, only that the Antichrist can't be unleashed until the Church is safely in heaven. That is how Paul calmed the Thessalonians—by *reminding* them of this sequence, not by saying that no one today can identify the Antichrist. (See Appendix C.)

A Stunning Contradiction — In addition to all of this evidence, let's consider one more thing: If the conventional wisdom is right about when the Antichrist will be identified, *then a major contradiction exists in the Word of God.* This is because—if the experts are right—the Antichrist will be "identified" at the very moment the Bible says his identity will be "concealed." The concealment of the Antichrist's true nature and identity immediately following the Rapture is well established in Scripture, and no expert disputes it:

- 2 Thessalonians 2:11 says that God is going to send a "**strong delusion**" to obscure the Beast's true nature and objectives.

- 2 Thessalonians 2: 9 says the Beast is going to perform "**lying wonders**" to fool the public and mask his identity.

- Revelation 13:3-4 says that people are going to "**wonder after**" the Beast and "**worship**" him as a god—not recoil from him as the son of hell.

- 2 Corinthians 4:4 says that during this whole time, Satan himself will **blind almost every person on earth to the truth**, including, no doubt, the truth about the man who will take center stage immediately following the Rapture.

Consequently, the experts have a major problem: If they acknowledge the verses above (as they should) and agree that the Antichrist's true nature is going to be *concealed* following the Rapture, then how can they insist that his identity is going to be "revealed" at the same time? How can both of those statements be true? What is the answer?

Well…if we go by what the experts have said, there is no answer.

However, if we go by the theme of this essay, the answer is simple. It's that the word *revealed* does not mean to be "identified." It means to be "unleashed," or to "rise up in power." And that's why Paul says in verse 2:2 that the Church has nothing to worry about! She will leave this planet before the Antichrist is *unleashed*, not before he's *identified*.

Therefore:

> **The word "revealed" in 2 Thessalonians cannot have anything to do with *disclosing an identity*. It cannot mean the Antichrist will suddenly be recognized as the Evil One after the Rapture. It has to mean he will suddenly be *unleashed* to reign on the earth and destroy mankind. That is the only way this riddle can be solved.**

And that fact is what allows us to solve the puzzle and place all the pieces in sequence:

- *First, Paul says, the Antichrist cannot <u>come to power</u> (be "revealed") until after the Rapture (2 Thess. 2:3 and 2:8).*

- *Then, Paul says, after the Rapture the Antichrist will be <u>unleashed</u> to rule "that day," "sit in the temple," do the "work of Satan," and perform "lying signs and wonders" (2 Thess. 2:3, 9).*

- *Yet, Paul says, his true identity will remain <u>hidden</u> from the masses, even after he steps into the spotlight, because God will send a strong <u>delusion</u> to keep the people in darkness. The Lord will give these rebels exactly what they want and turn them over to their god (2 Thess. 2:4, 2:9, and 2:11).*

Or to put it another way, Paul simply teaches that:

- First, the Church will be <u>raptured</u> (*taken out of the way*).

- Then the Antichrist can <u>come to power</u> (*be revealed*).

- Then the people who have rejected Christ and remain upon the earth <u>will be fooled</u> by that monster and worship him (*they'll be deluded by Satan and blinded by the Lord.*)

Hence, both context and logic prove that Paul never said the Church cannot learn the identity of the Antichrist. He simply said that the Antichrist cannot come to power until the Church is out of the way. Any other interpretation results in a major contradiction within the Word of God. And we know that's just not possible.

No Corroboration — One final point deserves mentioning. People who study the Bible know that any interpretation of Scripture must pass several tests before that interpretation can be regarded as true.

One such test is the existence of at least two separate passages that specifically confirm the teaching in question:

> **Deuteronomy 19:15** – [A]t the mouth of two...or...three witnesses, shall the matter be established.

In light of this principle, most expositors hesitate to characterize any interpretation as true, if that interpretation is based on a single section of Scripture. Failure to corroborate a given position with at least two unambiguous verses is a recipe for error.

Therefore, those who insist that Paul said the Antichrist cannot be identified until after the Rapture have a serious problem, because aside from an incorrect reading of Second Thessalonians, there is no passage in God's Word which makes such a statement, or even implies it. The corroboration required by Deuteronomy 19 just doesn't exist. The Bible never says: "The Church cannot learn the identity of the Antichrist." (See next item.)

2. The Bible never says the Antichrist's identity is off-limits to the Church.

Many people believe that somewhere in Scripture there's a verse that says the Church is not permitted to know the identity of the Beast. Somewhere, they say, there's a passage that outlaws such knowledge. Yet nothing could be further from the truth. Not one verse in Scripture states that the Church is prohibited from learning the identity of the Antichrist. Not one.

This is significant. If such an important topic was truly outside the realm of "approved" Church knowledge, the Holy Spirit almost certainly would have said so somewhere in the Apocalypse or in the First Epistle of John (the letter which introduces the word "antichrist" as a pseudonym for the Beast.) But no such taboo or restriction appears in the Apocalypse or anywhere else in God's Word.

In fact, the Bible doesn't even prohibit the Church from *attempting* to look for the Antichrist. Instead, the decision to search for that person has been left to our discretion.

This explains why so many of the early church fathers, and even several leaders of the Protestant Reformation, openly and repeatedly tried to identify the Man of Sin. They wrote at length on this topic and prayed for understanding because they knew this activity was neither prohibited nor pointless.

For example, Hippolytus of Rome (170–235 A.D.) advised the brethren: "It is proper that we take the Holy Scriptures in hand and find out...What his [the Antichrist's] name is."

At about the same time, Irenaeus of Lyon (130–202 A.D.) tried to identify the Antichrist, but failed. He then cautioned against wild speculation, noting that many names could add to 666. Yet he never said the Bible prohibits a search for the Beast, or that the Beast's identity could not be learned till after the Rapture.

About 200 years later, Augustine of Hippo (354–430 A.D.) claimed that Nero was the Antichrist. So did Jerome of Stridon (347–420 A.D.)

Indeed, quite a few champions of the faith, both during and after the Protestant Reformation—Martin Luther, John Wesley, Francis Turretin, Charles Spurgeon, and others—insisted the pope was the Antichrist. They were wrong about the Antichrist's identity, of course. But it is doubtful these erudite Christians would have studied the matter or published their opinions, had they not believed it was both permissible and possible to identify the Man of Sin today.

By contrast, when the Holy Spirit wants to prevent the Church from speculating on a subject, he draws a bright line. In Revelation 10:4, for example, John was *specifically* warned not to write what the Seven Thunders had said. John, of course, complied with that order, and wise Christians don't speculate on the matter.

Again, in Matthew 24, verses 36 and 44, Jesus *specifically* tells us that no one can know the date of the Rapture—not even the month or the year. So it is pointless to try and figure it out. That is not what Jesus wants the Church to be doing.

Yet, significantly, a similar admonition against researching the identity of the Antichrist is never recorded anywhere in the Word of God. Nowhere does the Bible say: "The Church must not look for the Antichrist."

3. The Bible never says that the Beast can't be identified until the Tribulation begins.

In addition to the fact that Scripture does not prohibit a *certain group* from learning the identity of the Antichrist (e.g., the Church), the Bible does not restrict that discovery to a *certain time period or epoch*. That is to say, there are no "blackout dates" regarding the knowledge of the Antichrist's identity. At least, not for the Church.

In fact, despite what many experts now teach, the Bible never says, *The Antichrist can only be identified after the Tribulation begins.* Nor does it say anything like, *The Beast can only be identified after he enters the Temple and declares himself to be God.*

Those who believe that Scripture makes such a statement usually cite Second Thessalonians 2:6-8 to make their case. However, as we just saw in Item 1, a thorough analysis of Second Thessalonians lends no support to that position. In fact, the "identification: impossible" doctrine that's derived from those verses must be reached by inference. It is never explicitly stated there or anywhere else.

Thus, not only is the identification of the Beast not off-limits to any *specific group* (such as the Church), but the identification of the Beast is not confined to any particular *moment of history* (such as after the Rapture). For the Church, it can just as easily happen before the start of the Tribulation as after, without violating any dates, timelines, or sequences in God's Word.

4. The Bible never says not even Satan can know who the Antichrist is.

One of the more recent arguments which has emerged to discourage the Church from looking for the Antichrist says that God has hidden the identity of the Antichrist so well that not even Satan can know who the Man of Sin is going to be.

Consequently, because of this "information black-out," the devil has been forced to groom a candidate in each generation for the position of Antichrist. He is then required to restart the process, once that candidate fails to become the Beast of the Apocalypse and dies. In this scenario, you see, someone must always be on standby to rule the world because Satan has no idea when the Tribulation will start. Thus (if we can believe this conjecture), there have been over two dozen Antichrist hopefuls over the last two thousand years — all of whom somehow have names that add to 666 — and the enemy must be quite frustrated by now!

(Indeed, if we take this idea to its logical conclusion, then we have to assume that Satan has *also* been grooming dozens of False Prophet candidates and hundreds of kings [for the ten-king alliance] over the same period—at which point the theory becomes completely absurd!)

To be sure, many evil dictators and kingpins have risen over the last two millennia. And 1 John 2:18 indeed says that many "antichrists" are now present (referring *not* to imaginary "trainees" for the position of Antichrist, but to false brethren who have left the Church and are now working against Jesus.) I will even admit that the "revolving-Antichrist" theory is clever. But this scenario has no foundation in Scripture. It is not based on anything that Jesus, John, or Paul actually said. It was created simply to keep the *No-one-can-know-who-the-Antichrist-is* doctrine intact. In truth, not one verse in the Bible suggests that Satan has been repeatedly locating and preparing Antichrist prospects since the days of the apostles.

Instead, the Apocalypse clearly portrays Satan (a.k.a., the Dragon) standing on a beach, patiently waiting for the *one-and-only* Antichrist, or "beast," to emerge from the Sea at the right moment in time:

> **Revelation 12:17, 13:1-2** (ESV) — Then the dragon [Satan] became furious with the woman [Israel] and went off to make war with the rest of her offspring [the Church] ... And he [Satan] stood on the sand of the sea. And I saw a beast [the Antichrist] rising out of the sea... And to it the dragon gave his power and his throne and great authority.

One dragon. One beast. One place. One moment. Just once.

Nevertheless, despite the fact that the here-and-then-gone Antichrist theory is entirely speculative, it has gained quite a bit of traction in the Church. And it's being used to quash any inquiry into the identity of the Man of Sin. After all, if Satan can't know who the Antichrist is, then we certainly can't.

In my opinion, however, a better hypothesis—and one that is actually supported by Scripture—is this: For the last two thousand years Satan has been waiting for permission (from heaven) to sire a son. Genesis 3:15 indicates the Antichrist will be the very *seed* of Satan, and Revelation 13:1 pictures the Dragon awaiting the birth of just *one individual* who is a carbon copy of himself (i.e., has seven heads, ten horns, scarlet coloring, and a visceral hatred for Christ.) Therefore, it is extremely unlikely that Satan has been interviewing and prepping a continuous line of Antichrist candidates over the last twenty centuries. Instead, it is far more likely the enemy has been waiting for permission to produce the seed that was mentioned in Genesis 3. He has been waiting to sire his one-and-only biological child. And that means, when the time is right, even without knowing the date of the Rapture, the devil will know exactly who the Antichrist is.

To my mind, this scenario—that the Antichrist is the enemy's one-and-only biological child—makes sense because, among other reasons (such as the enemy's insatiable desire to imitate God), the Antichrist must be the *legal heir* to Satan's kingdom in order to receive mankind's worship on Satan's behalf (Rev. 13:4). And that, in turn, requires the Antichrist to be his physical offspring.

If this is correct—and I believe it is—then Satan will know exactly who the Antichrist is. And that means several other individuals will know who he is, as well, a fact which then opens the door for the Church to know. (See Item 11.)

As a bonus, this scenario keeps the doctrine of imminence intact because, even after the Antichrist is born and begins to mature, neither the devil nor anyone else will know the date of the Rapture. The devil will simply know that the final countdown has started and the time for the Rapture is near, something which all of Christendom has known since Israel became a nation again in 1948. (Please see next item.)

5. Imminence does not prevent the Church from learning the Antichrist's identity.

In the midst of Jesus's longest discourse on end-time events, our Lord told the disciples that no one but God can know the date of the Rapture. The Church must therefore be ready for it at all times.

This is called the doctrine of imminence, and it's based on Matthew 24:36: "But of that day and hour knoweth no man, no, not the angels of heaven, but my Father only."

Verse 42 is similar and completes the concept: "Watch therefore: for ye know not what hour your Lord doth come [at the Rapture]."

In other words, if I might paraphrase, the call to heaven can happen at any moment. There are no signs—such as the identification of the Antichrist—which have to precede the Rapture. Therefore, we must always be ready for the "last trump" to sound. The Rapture literally could happen in the very next second.

As a result, expositors often make two arguments against knowing the identity of the Antichrist, based on these verses.

The first argument says: If we learned who the Antichrist was, we would then have a pretty good idea of the "day" and "hour" of Jesus' return for the Church. We would know the approximate date of the Rapture and the start of the Tribulation—or, at least, we'd know the latest date by which those events must occur.[8] In that case, imminence would be destroyed and the verses above would be violated. (At least, so goes the argument.)

---

[8]   If we knew who the Antichrist was—and thus, the year he was born—the Rapture would have to occur at least seven years before the normal lifespan of that man was reached. According to Psalm 90:10, a man is typically allotted 70–80 years. And, interestingly enough, the actuarial tables for Italy currently show the average lifespan of a man is about 80 years. Therefore, the Rapture would have to occur no later than (about) the Antichrist's 73rd birthday (plus or minus a few years).

But is that true? I will admit, at first blush, this argument appears to carry some weight. It seems to apply the words of Christ in a consistent and rational manner. If we knew who the Antichrist was, we would certainly know that the Rapture was near. We would know the Rapture would occur in our lifetime. However, this argument is not as foolproof as some might think, because upon closer analysis we find it contains an error in logic. And that error is critical.

Specifically: Information of a general nature cannot be extrapolated to determine the exact timing of anything. Or to say it another way, knowing the Antichrist is alive might tell us the Tribulation is near. It might even tell us the Rapture will occur in our lifetime. But it wouldn't tell us the precise date of the Rapture or the starting point of the twenty-one Judgments. The exact timing of those events would still be unknown—*even after learning the identity of the Antichrist*—and we would still have to live as though the Rapture could happen at any moment. The Rapture would still be imminent. And that means the doctrine of *imminence* would remain intact.[9]

* * * *

As for the second imminence-based argument, it can be summarized as follows: If any verse of Scripture taught that the Antichrist *must be* identified prior to the Rapture, then none of the passages which state that Christ's return for the Church is able to happen at any moment could possibly be true.

Instead, the Antichrist would *first* have to be identified before Jesus could come back, and that means the so-called "imminent" Rapture would no longer be "imminent." In fact, every time that Jesus said the Rapture could happen at any moment, he would've been undermining some other portion of Scripture. And that is unthinkable.

So...how do we resolve this dilemma? What is the answer?

---

9   Incidentally, we have known the Rapture will occur in our lifetime (our "generation") since 1948 when Israel (the "fig tree") became a nation again (Mt. 24:32-33).

Well, if the Bible taught that the identification of the Antichrist *had to* occur prior to the Rapture, then imminence would indeed be destroyed. No doubt about it. If the Antichrist *had to be identified first*, then the Rapture could not happen suddenly and without warning. Instead, we would have to wait for the discovery of the Antichrist to take place before we could even hope to see the Rapture.

I therefore concede the point: Nothing in God's Word says the Antichrist *must be* identified today.

However…while Scripture does not say the Antichrist *must be* identified today, neither does the Bible *rule it out*. Instead, the Bible leaves that question completely unanswered. It never specifies when that identification will take place. And that means—even if the Antichrist was discovered right now—the doctrine of imminence would not be violated, because that event is simply a possibility, not a requirement. It can happen just as easily before the Rapture, as after, without violating any date, sequence, or doctrine in God's Word.

* * * *

In short, neither aspect of imminence (above) actually prevents the Church from identifying the Antichrist today: if we knew who the Antichrist was, we *still* wouldn't know the exact date of the Rapture, which means we *still* would have to live as though it could happen at any moment. And just because Scripture *allows* us to identify the Antichrist prior to the Rapture, it doesn't mean he *has to* be identified—a fact which still leaves the doctrine of imminence intact.

6. Acts 1:7 does not prevent the Church from learning the identity of the Antichrist.

Just before Jesus ascended back to heaven, the disciples asked him if he would immediately restore Israel as an *independent kingdom,* in accordance with the prophecies which mark the start of the last days.

Jesus responded to their question by saying: "It is not for you to know **the times or the seasons**, which the Father hath put in his own power" (Acts 1:7).

Many expositors cite this as proof that the Church cannot learn the identity of the Antichrist until after the Rapture: If we knew who the Antichrist was, we would then know that the **"times and seasons"** were upon us—something which Jesus had declared off-limits to speculation. So how do we proceed?

The dilemma is certainly quite interesting. The Master's rebuke definitely applied to the disciples, and to the generations of Christians that followed. None of us are supposed to know in advance when the last days will start. That is beyond question.

Still, most rules have an expiration date. And in this case the injunction against knowing when the last days will start ended in 1948, because that's when the disciples' question was incontrovertibly answered by the restoration of Israel as an *independent kingdom.*

At that point, the end times were officially inaugurated (i.e., the "times and seasons" to which Jesus referred in the first chapter of Acts.) And thus, for the last seventy years it has been the *duty* of Christians to not only recognize the season of which Jesus spoke, but to discern all the signs leading up to the Rapture, including (possibly) the identity of the Antichrist:

> **Luke 12:56 – Ye hypocrites,** ye can discern the face of the sky and of the earth; but how is it that **ye do not discern this time?**

> **Matthew 24:33-34 –** So likewise ye, when ye shall see all these things [including the rise of **false christs** mentioned in verse 5], know that it is **near,** even at the doors. Verily I say unto you, This generation shall not pass, till all these things be fulfilled.

Luke 21:28 – But when these things begin to come to pass, look up, and lift up your heads; because your redemption **[the Rapture] draweth nigh.**

In plain language, Jesus says that any Christian who fails to look for the signs of the last days and to recognize each one as it appears, is not only a "hypocrite" (to the extent he or she studies and accepts the legitimacy of other signs, such as those of an impending rainstorm), but is missing out on the joy and purifying effect of knowing that our Lord's return is at the door.

Indeed, since Jesus said it is our duty to be looking for *all* of the signs of his coming—including the rise of "**false christs**" (Mt. 24:5)—then perhaps instead of *avoiding* a search for the greatest false christ in history, we should actually be *looking* for him!

7. Past failures to identify the Antichrist do not preclude identifying him now.

The final argument that's used to discourage the Church from determining the Antichrist's identity goes something like this:

> *For the last two thousand years, every attempt to name the Antichrist has failed. Obviously, this means that God has been deflecting our attempts to locate the Man of Sin and it is pointless to keep on trying. God will not allow anyone to learn the name of the Beast until the Rapture takes place. And that's that!*

Interestingly, the vast majority of prophecy experts agree with this statement (to one degree or another.) And they have an enormous amount of precedent on their side. Not only has the real Antichrist failed to materialize at any point in time, but he doesn't seem to be anywhere on the horizon, either. At least, no individual seems to meet all the qualifications at this moment.

However, the mere fact that no despot over the last twenty centuries has turned out to be the Antichrist cannot be cited, in and of itself, as proof that he can't be identified until after the Rapture. Nor does it prove that God doesn't want us to know. Past failures to identify someone do not necessarily mean that person is destined to remain hidden until some future event.

Instead, the only conclusions that logically may be drawn are:

- The person in question has not yet arrived, or

- The investigators lack the proper information, or

- The investigators are misinterpreting the information, or

- The investigators are concentrating on the wrong suspect.

In other words, the mere fact that people have misidentified the Antichrist before, doesn't necessarily mean that individual is forever immune to discovery. For example, when the Jewish leaders and Zealots of the First and Second Centuries repeatedly misidentified their Messiah, it wasn't because God hadn't told them, or because he didn't want them to know, or because a certain prophetic event had yet to take place. It was because the leaders of Israel, in their pride and jealousy, refused to apply the relevant prophecies to Jesus. Instead, they rejected the "upstart" rabbi from Nazareth and began to concentrate on all the wrong candidates. It's as simple as that.

Consequently: *It indeed may be* that the Antichrist will not be identified until after the Rapture. But the mere fact that no one has yet been able to identify the Antichrist, doesn't automatically translate into a proof of that position. At least, not if we're going to abide by the rules of logic.

* * * *

Please see **Appendix B** for additional evidence that nothing in Scripture prohibits the Church from discovering the identity of the Antichrist.

SECTION II – *GOD SAVES PEOPLE FROM JUDGMENT BY REVEALING THE DETAILS OF PROPHECY IN ADVANCE*

IN THE PREVIOUS SECTION we learned that nothing in the Bible prohibits the Church from *looking* for the Antichrist, or from actually *learning* his identity.

It is therefore time to consider how God has used prophecy in the past to help people escape judgment *and* whether discovering the Antichrist's identity—if, in fact, that happens—might be another example of God helping people to escape the coming storm.

 # 8. The Lord *always* warns people of impending judgment so they have a chance to escape.

Throughout the Bible, whenever a person or nation had exhausted God's patience and proved they were deserving of judgment, God never sent his wrath without first providing a warning. From Cain to Pharaoh, and Nebuchadnezzar to Herod, the Lord never punished anyone until he had pleaded with the offender to change his ways.

Take a look at the chart below and notice how many times God attempted to spare people's lives by first providing a warning:

43

PROPHET and PREDICTION	RESULT
Noah - Impending flood **2 Peter 2:5**	Noah's family saved **Genesis 8**
Angels - Destruction of Sodom and Gomorrah **Genesis 19:13**	Lot and his family saved **Genesis 19:29**
Joseph - 7 years of famine in Egypt **Genesis 41:30**	Egypt and Joseph's family saved **Genesis 47:11**
Moses - Plagues against Egypt **Exodus 6:6-9**	All Hebrews saved **Exodus 12:31-42**
Jonah - God's coming wrath on Nineveh **Jonah 3:1-4**	All Nineveh saved **Jonah 3:10**
Jeremiah - Babylonian invasion **Jeremiah 20**	Precious few saved **Daniel 1:1-2**
Jesus - Future siege of Jerusalem **Luke 21:20-21**	Thousands will be saved **Daniel 12:1**

The Scriptures say that God is slow to anger and quick to forgive. He wants to save people, not destroy them. He is not willing that any should perish, but that all should come to repentance. God therefore tells us when judgment is near. And he always uses detailed prophecy to get the job done.

In fact, as you can see from our chart, providing people with detailed predictions has been an integral part of God's plan for saving them throughout history. It's his standard operating procedure.

Consequently, the idea that the identity of the Antichrist might be revealed today is fully consistent with the Lord's "prophecy protocol." It's the kind of revelation that could easily fit in the preceding chart, because it would prove the Tribulation is right at our doorstep, and thus, it would convince thousands of people that judgment was coming. It would serve as a wake-up call to the Church. And that, in turn, would cause us to get serious about winning the lost. It would motivate us to walk in holiness and "do the right thing." It would inspire us to review our teachings and correct false doctrine. It would spur us to prayer, fasting, worship, and evangelization.

The revelation of the Antichrist's identity is therefore likely to occur before the Tribulation, because that's when such an event could save the most people from judgment. And we know that saving people from judgment is God's most passionate objective:

> **John 3:16-17** – For God so loved the world, that he gave his only begotten Son, that whosoever believeth in him should not perish, but have everlasting life. For God sent not his Son into the world to condemn the world; but that the world through him might be saved.

> **1 Timothy 2:4** – For this is good and acceptable in the sight of God our Savior; Who will have all men to be saved, and to come unto the knowledge of the truth.

9. The Lord sometimes names *key individuals* years in advance of their birth, so believers will know when the critical moment has arrived.

Here is something not too many Christians are aware of: God sometimes saves people by naming biblical "VIPs" hundreds of years before they appear!

That might seem hard to believe, but just consider all of the people whom Scripture named over a century in advance of their arrival:

- Jesus, a.k.a., "Joshua" (Zech. 3:1)

- Jesus the "Nazarene" (Is. 11:1, Jer. 23:5, Zech. 6:12)

- King "Cyrus" of Persia (Is. 44:28–45:1)

- King "Josiah" of Israel (I Kings 13:2)

- "Mary," the mother of Jesus (Ruth 1:20, *mara* of Bethlehem)

These examples demonstrate two important concepts. First, they show that the Bible is reliable, because only an all-knowing God could name people centuries before they were born.

And second, they prove that God is willing to reveal the names of certain individuals, if that revelation will help people to escape an impending calamity, or even the Final Judgment.

In naming King Cyrus, for example, the Jews knew which king they could trust when the command to rebuild Jerusalem was issued.

In naming Jesus of Nazareth, the Jews knew (or at least, it was intended for them to know) which man was the promised Messiah, and therefore which person they could trust to save them from God's wrath.

But does this pattern of *naming names* extend to the Antichrist?

I believe it does.

In the first place, speaking under the inspiration of the Holy Spirit, the prophet Amos once declared that God never makes a major move on the stage of history without first revealing his secrets:

> **Amos 3:7** – Surely the Lord God will do nothing, but **he revealeth his secret** unto his servants the prophets.

Before God acts, he tells his people what will happen. He gives them the *inside track* on future events. He tells them the time, place, and outcome of looming developments so they can escape a major disaster. God did this, for example, when he told Noah that a world-wide flood was coming. The Lord did it again when he told Joseph that a seven-year famine was about to hit Egypt. The Lord did it once more when he told Moses that ten plagues were about to strike the land of the Pharaohs.

Therefore, if God decides to give us the name of the Antichrist today, it would simply be an extension of the pattern which God has already set. It would simply be another instance of God extending his grace and mercy before unleashing his wrath upon the earth. It would be another case of God unlocking a big "secret," and "naming a name," in order to save people from judgment.

In fact, if God was to name the Antichrist today, that revelation *unlike anything else* would confirm that Satan's man is actually alive, and that time is short. There would no longer be any question that the Rapture was just moments away.

The result? Untold thousands would surrender to Christ! Pastors would then have a new and exciting task on their hands, as scores of fresh believers began swarming the sanctuaries to learn what they should do next. The Church itself would be compelled to renew its commitment to prayer, fasting, and worship!

> **Hebrews 10:24-25** (NKJV) – And let us consider one another in order to **stir up love and good works**, not forsaking the assembling of ourselves together, as *is* the manner of some, but exhorting one another, and so much the more **as you see the Day approaching**.

Therefore, while none of these scriptures specifically say that God will reveal the name of the Antichrist today, they prove that such a revelation, if it occurred, would be totally *consistent* with God's method for saving people from judgment. (And that's all we're looking for at this point in our thesis.)

In the meantime, here's what we need to take from this discussion:

1. God sometimes **names the names** of biblical VIPs years before they come to the forefront.

2. God never makes a move on the stage of history without first revealing his most **incredible secrets**.

3. If God revealed the name of the Antichrist now, he would simply be doing what he has done throughout history: **naming a name** and revealing an **incredible secret**.

Let's continue…

10. God reveals hidden things to "kings."

Speaking under the inspiration of the Holy Spirit, Solomon once declared that God expects His people to discern the meaning of prophecy:

> **Proverbs 25:2** – It is the glory of God to **conceal a thing**:
> but the honour of **kings** is to search out a matter.

This verse is so brief that one could easily miss the significance of what Solomon was saying. But this is one verse that should *not* be overlooked. Why? Because this verse declares that it's an honor to decipher God's mysteries. And that means God *wants us* to "search out" his riddles, including things like the renowned 666 code.

Moreover, it is indisputable that these words apply to the Church, as well as to monarchs, because the word "kings" refers not just to political rulers and dynasties, but also to faithful believers in Christ.

The New Testament makes it clear that God sees His people as "kings and priests":

> **Revelation 1:4-6** — Grace be unto you, and peace...from Jesus Christ...that loved us, and washed us from our sins in his own blood, **And hath made us kings and priests** unto God.

> **Revelation 2:26** — And he that overcometh, and keepeth my works unto the end, to him will **I give power over the nations**.

> **Luke 19:17** — And he said unto him, Well, thou good servant: because thou hast been faithful in a very little, have thou **authority over ten cities**.

Thus, taken together, these verses prove that even the most sensitive prophetic issues—such as the name and identity of the Antichrist—are not off-limits to pastors, teachers, or the Christian community in general. Instead, God expects his "kings" to thoroughly search out his mysteries and to make an attempt to determine their meaning. The study and interpretation of *every aspect* of God's prophetic Word should be a normal part of the Christian life.

Indeed, not only do we have God's blessings to study and solve these kinds of enigmas, but it actually upsets the Lord when we fail to try!

The story recorded in Luke 19:41-44 makes the point. Here, we learn that Jesus actually *wept* because the Jewish leadership had failed to study the prophecies of Daniel 9, and therefore had failed to calculate the date of the Messiah's arrival in 32 A.D. (that is, 483 "prophetic years" after 445 B.C.) [10]

---

[10] For an analysis of the 70 Weeks prophecy and the timing of Messiah's arrival, see *The Coming Prince*, by Robert Anderson (1895).

As a result, the Sanhedrin did not know the "time of their visitation" and ended up rejecting the only man on earth who could've saved them from the looming Roman onslaught:

> **Luke 19:41-44** — And when he [Jesus] drew near and saw the city, he **wept** over it, saying, **"Would that you, even you, had known on this day the things that make for peace!** But now they are hidden from your eyes. For the days will come upon you, when **your enemies will set up a barricade around you** and surround you and hem you in on every side and tear you down to the ground, you and your children within you. And they will not leave one stone upon another in you, **because you did not know the time of your visitation."**

God will send no new prophetic *revelation,* but he has promised to send greater *illumination* as the time of testing approaches (Dan. 12:9-10). Nothing can be added to the Scriptures. But God will give us greater understanding of those Scriptures as we approach the end of the age (Dan. 12:10).

God will do this because, as Peter once said, "The Lord is...not willing that any should perish, but that all should come to repentance" (2 Peter 3:9).

It is therefore quite possible that God will reveal the identity of the Antichrist today, because a revelation of that magnitude would dispel any doubt that the Tribulation was near. And that, in turn, would motivate thousands of people to escape the coming terror.

As the Lord once cautioned: "For **nothing is secret**, that shall not be **made manifest**; neither **any thing hid**, that shall not be **known and come abroad**. Take heed therefore how ye hear..." (Luke 8:17-18).

SECTION III – *THE LORD WANTS THE CHURCH TO BREAK THE 666 CODE*

THUS FAR we have demonstrated two of the three elements of our thesis:

A. Nothing in Scripture prohibits the identification of the Antichrist today.

B. God routinely saves people by providing—and decoding—detailed prophecies.

With these two foundations now firmly established, we are ready to consider the third and final part of our thesis, specifically, the part which says it is not only *possible* to identify the Antichrist, but that God actually *expects* us to make the attempt. (And believe it or not, the Lord has provided all of the tools required to do so, as we'll see in chapter 5.)

Here we go…

11. Certain people *absolutely* will know the identity of the Antichrist before the Rapture takes place.

Here is an interesting fact: Long before anyone else knew who Jesus really was, the true identity of the Messiah was known to several people around him. These individuals included Mary and Joseph, Elisabeth and Zacharias, the shepherds of Bethlehem, the Magi from the East, Anna, Simeon, John the Baptist, and, of course, the disciples of Galilee. Each of these people had been told on various occasions and through various means that Jesus of Nazareth was the promised Messiah. Each of these men and women then made it their goal to help raise him, bless him, teach him, or protect him, and then carry his message to the rest of the world.

Similarly, it is all but certain that a number of people in the enemy's camp will be recruited to help raise the Antichrist and prepare him for his ultimate role. And that means each of those individuals will know the identity of the Antichrist long before anyone else does. These will include the Antichrist's parents, his spouse, his personal staff, his political inner circle, his mentors, certain financial backers, the False Prophet, and possibly a handful of Catholic leaders.[11] How else could an otherwise insignificant "nobody"[12] suddenly obtain international power? That is just common sense.

But that's not all. The fact that certain people in the enemy's camp will know *who the Antichrist is* actually opens the door for us to know, as well! Why? Because once the enemy knows the identity of the Antichrist, an extraordinary principle comes into play—a principle that only a handful of people are aware of.

What is that principle? It is simply this: The Lord sometimes makes a mockery of the enemy by passing the enemy's most well-guarded secrets to faithful believers!

You read that correctly. The Lord, on occasion, actually makes sport of the enemy by telling believers exactly what the enemy is doing—and through whom the enemy is working!

Here are just a few examples of this principle in action:

> **2 Kings 6:11-12** (NIV) – This enraged the king of Aram. He summoned his officers and demanded of them, "Tell me! Which of us is on the side of the king of Israel?" "None of us, my lord the king," said one of his officers,

---

[11] The proposition that certain Vatican leaders might already know the Antichrist's identity finds general support in several popular exposés. See, for example, Malachi Martin, *The Keys of This Blood* (New York: Simon & Schuster, 1991), p. 632. Also see Thomas Horn and Chris Putnam, *Petrus Romanus: The Final Pope is Here* (Crane, MO: Defender, 2012), pp. 91-94, 96, 442-443.

[12] Several scriptures imply the Antichrist will rise suddenly from obscurity as a commoner. These include Dan. 7:8 (the "little horn"), Dan. 8:9 (the "little horn"), and Dan. 11:21 (the "vile person, to whom they shall not give the honour of the kingdom.")

"but Elisha, the prophet who is in Israel, tells the king of Israel the very words you speak in your bedroom."

Jeremiah 11:18 (NIV) – Because the Lord revealed their plot to me, I knew it, for at that time he showed me what they were doing.

Matthew 2:12 (NIV/KJV) – On coming to the house, they [the Wise Men] saw the child with his mother Mary, and they bowed down and worshiped him. Then they opened their treasures and presented him with gifts of gold, frankincense and myrrh. And having been warned in a dream not to go back to Herod, they returned to their country by another route... Then Herod, when he saw that he was mocked of the wise men, was exceeding wroth.

Consequently, in light of all these precedents—plus a bit of common sense regarding the Antichrist's "sudden" rise to power—the claim, by some, that no one can know the identity of the Antichrist until the Church disappears is flat mistaken.

Instead, the enemy and several of his comrades *will know* that secret. And because they'll know it, and because God takes so much pleasure in humiliating the enemy, it is entirely possible that God will trump the enemy once again by relaying that very piece of "classified information"—the identity of the Antichrist—to the Church.

In fact, from my point of view, it is not only *possible* that we will learn the name of the Antichrist, it is highly *probable*. And I believe we will learn it just before we're raptured to heaven.

This is especially true since Jeremiah the prophet said that God is willing to show us "great and mighty things" about prophecy, if we will only ask. (See next item.)

12. God reveals incredible secrets to those who ask.

Believe it or not, the Bible contains over one hundred prophecies regarding the Antichrist and his exploits.[13] In fact, aside from Jesus of Nazareth, there are more prophecies about this individual than any other character in Scripture. Clearly, this isn't the kind of emphasis one would expect, if the Lord intended to keep the identity of the Antichrist from the Church.

Indeed, the amount of "Antichrist detail" contained in Scripture is staggering! Just consider a few of those details below, and then ask yourself: Why would God divulge so much information about one individual, if not to *reveal* that person to those who study his Word?

Here are just six things that God has told us about the Antichrist. (And note that each one can be used to narrow the search for this monster today.) According to Scripture, the Antichrist will:

- Rise as a peace negotiator (Dan. 8:25: 9:27)

- Come from a place to the northwest of Israel (Dan. 8:9)

- Perform lying signs and wonders (2 Thess. 2:9)

- Have a name that adds to 666 (Rev. 13:18)

- Emerge from the Roman people (Dan. 9:26)

- Revile the faithful of Israel (Dan. 7:25)

Keep in mind that the above data represents just a tiny fraction of the total amount contained in Scripture regarding the Antichrist. There are actually over a hundred more data-points that describe this character. The Bible is filled with this "Antichrist information."

---

[13] Please see *The Antichrist* (coming in late 2023).

Yet despite all of these details, many pastors and scholars say we shouldn't expect to see the man who will actually fulfill these descriptions. It's okay to study those verses and guess at their meaning. But we shouldn't raise our hopes about using that data to identify the Man of Sin or to solve the 666 code. At least, not until after the Rapture, they say.

But does that really make sense? And, more importantly, is that what the Word of God actually teaches? No, it is not! In fact, far from prohibiting a search for the Antichrist, the Holy Spirit promises to reveal these kinds of mysteries, provided we make our petitions in earnest. All we have to do is ask!

Read the following verse and decide for yourself:

> **Jeremiah 33:3** – Call unto me, and **I will answer thee**, and show thee **great and mighty things**, which thou knowest not.

It would be hard to make this much clearer. If we call to the Lord and ask him to show us his mysteries—mysteries like the 666 code—*he will answer* and show us "great and mighty things" about them. Things we think are so far out of reach, we dare not even consider them. Things we "knowest not."

This verse alone suggests that learning the identity of the Antichrist is not altogether impossible, because God has placed no restrictions on what he is willing to show us. He has not said, *I will show thee great and mighty things—except the identity of the Antichrist!* Instead, he has said, *Call unto me, and I will answer thee, and show thee great and mighty things, which thou knowest not.*

That's a pretty broad and inclusive statement. It doesn't leave much room for exceptions. And God is the one who said it! So perhaps we should take God at his word and ask him to show us great and mighty things about the Anti-messiah. Things like the 666 code (Rev. 13:18), or perhaps his blasphemous name (Rev. 13:1), or maybe even the identity of his sidekick, the False Prophet (Rev. 13:11).

Indeed, in my estimation, God is already beginning to pull back the curtain on prophecies like this. Ever since 1948 and the rebirth of Israel, God has illuminated more details about the Beast and his empire than ever before. For example, as of today, the following things about this man have been established with a very high degree of confidence:

- Nationality – Italian

- Religion – Roman Catholic

- Military force – European Intervention Initiative (EI2)

- 666 Mark – Implantable chips, RFIDs, recombinant DNA

- Global government – The United Nations and its agencies

- Physical appearance – Augustus, Tiberius, Caligula, Claudius, or Nero[14]

In view of these specifics, plus the scores of additional Antichrist prophecies and narratives to which I alluded in the first paragraph, plus the extended list of names and titles that have been assigned to the Beast, *plus* the tantalizing "666" code, can we honestly believe that God doesn't want the Church to solve the mystery of the Beast? Can we really believe that all of this information exists simply to tease us, or that God has suddenly decided to stop divulging "great and mighty things" about the Antichrist just when the Rapture is about to take place, or that God is going to leave the analysis of all this information to apostates and backsliders who will miss the Rapture and be struggling day-to-day just to survive the Tribulation?

---

[14] Please see *Empire of the Antichrist* (Positron Books, 2020).

Of course not! God gave *the Church* hundreds of details regarding the Beast, and he is continuing to send the explanations. As the Lord told Jeremiah centuries ago, heaven will continue to peel back the layers of prophecy in the last days, so that mankind can see exactly what is approaching and have a chance to repent:

> **Jeremiah 23:20** (NIV) – The **anger of the Lord** will not turn back until he fully accomplishes the purposes of his heart. In days to come **you will understand it clearly**.

Without question, God will continue to unlock the meaning of end-time prophecy until we "understand it clearly." That was the teaching of Jeremiah, as well as Amos, John, Daniel, and many other prophets.[15] And that information must include every major detail that pertains to the Beast, because no exclusions are listed.

In evidence, consider this statement which was made by an Angel of the Lord just before he gave Daniel some of the most specific characteristics regarding the Antichrist:

> **Daniel 10:12-14** – Fear not, Daniel: for from the first day that thou didst set thine heart to understand…thy words were heard… Now I am come to make thee understand what shall befall thy people in the latter days.

The Angel then proceeded to list such things as the Antichrist's:

- **Social status** – a commoner (v. 11:21)

- **Personality** – predatorial and full of greed (v. 11:25, 28)

- **Theater of operations** – North Africa, the Mediterranean, the Middle East (v. 11:25, 30, 41, 42)

- **Self-deification** – claims to be God (v. 11:36, 37)

---

[15] Amos 3:7, John 16:13, Dan. 12:10, etc.

- **Religion** – the worship of a god of fortresses (v. 11:38, 39)

The lesson? When we "set our hearts to understand" prophecy, God is gracious and sends us the answers until we "understand it clearly." That is the Lord's *modus operandi*. That is what he has said he will do. God wants his people to know about the future so they can be ready for it, and he uses detailed prophecy to get the job done.

Therefore, in view of everything that God has said about intending to unpack the layers of prophecy the closer we get to the end, only one conclusion is possible: God almost certainly intends to complete the picture of end-time prophecy by providing us with the identity of the Antichrist before the Tribulation begins. All we have to do is ask.

13. The Church will be guided into all truth concerning the last days.

In the Gospel of John, Jesus explicitly says that the Holy Spirit will guide the Church into all truth concerning the end times:

> **John 16:13** – How be it when he, the Spirit of truth, is come, he will guide **you** into **all truth**...and he will show you **things to come.**

This is a powerful statement. And, while it does not specifically say that God will reveal the identity of the Antichrist at the present time, can we, as Christians, honestly believe that "all truth" concerning "things to come" somehow excludes one of the most important elements of the last days, namely, the identity of the Beast?

Even Daniel said that as the Tribulation approached, God would bring more and more clarity to end-time predictions:

> **Daniel 12:9-10** – And he [the Angel] said, Go thy way, Daniel: for the words are closed up and sealed **till the time**

of the end. Many shall be purified, and made white, and tried; but the wicked shall do wickedly: and none of the wicked shall understand; **but the wise shall understand.**

These words, though recorded some twenty-six hundred years ago, can hardly be clearer. God promised that, as the Tribulation drew near, he would provide greater and greater insight into such topics as the Judgments, the Beast, the False Prophet, and the Whore of Babylon.

And the Lord has kept that promise! Just think of all the end-time predictions that God has already unlocked for the Church. For example, through the grace and power of the Holy Spirit, we now know the following things with a very high degree of certainty:

- **The ethnicities of the Satanic duo** – Rev. 13 and 17
  Italian Antichrist / *Jewish* False Prophet

- **The hope of the Church** – Rev. 4:1
  Raptured *before* the Judgments begin

- **The timeframe** – Mt. 24:34
  Within one generation of 1948 (Israel's rebirth)

- **The number of Tribulation deaths** – Mt. 24:22; Rev. 6:8, 9:1
  Over 7 billion people (a staggering tragedy!)

- **The Whore of Babylon** – Rev. 17:18
  The city of Rome

- **The mark of the Beast** – Rev. 13:16-17, 14:9-11
  Implantable chips, electronic tattoos, recombinant DNA

- **The futuristic capabilities of man** – Revelation 6, 7, 8, 9, 11, 13

  Television, GPS, the Internet, Robots, Weapons of Mass Destruction, Artificial Intelligence, etc.

In light of all the incredible details that God has already empowered the Church to decode, plus the Lord's promise to guide us into "all truth" concerning "things to come," it is difficult to see how the Lord could *not* allow us to spot the Antichrist. This is especially true since God has framed the Antichrist's identity in the form of a riddle—and riddles are always meant to be solved by the recipient. (See next item.)

14. Riddles are meant to be solved by the recipient.

No person deliberately sends a riddle to someone, unless the sender wants that recipient to solve it. People don't send pointless enigmas, and neither does God.

Whenever a riddle appears in a work of literature, whether it is the Bible, a Shakespearean play, or a dime-store novel, the author intends his audience to solve it. Indeed, the author is *daring* his audience to solve it.

This device is one of the most powerful means for drawing our attention to a critical issue and making it stick in our minds. Far from discouraging further inquiry, a riddle actually begs the reader to work the solution.

The famous riddle that Samson posed at his wedding celebration is but one example in Scripture:

> **Judges 14:14** – [Riddle] Out of the eater came forth meat, and out of the strong came forth sweetness.

Judges 14:18 – [Solution] What is sweeter than <u>honey</u>?
And what is stronger than a <u>lion</u>?

Although Samson's guests solved the riddle by cheating, Samson nevertheless rewarded his guests for their "accomplishment" because he *wanted* them to try to find the solution.

Similarly, since God has openly framed the identity of the Antichrist in the form of a riddle—i.e., the renowned 666 code—and since that riddle is specifically addressed to the Church, only one conclusion is possible: God wants the Church to determine the identity of the Beast. In fact, God is *daring* the Church to identify him, because we are the ones who own that enigma! (See next item.)

15. The 666 code belongs to the Church.

The intended recipient of the 666 code is the Church, that is, the body of believers who belong to Christ before the Rapture takes place. We know this is true because both Jesus and John repeatedly address the book of Revelation, in whole and in part, *exclusively* to the Church. No other recipient is even mentioned:

> **Revelation 1:4** – John **to the seven churches** which are in Asia.

> **Revelation 1:11** – What thou seest, write in a book, and **send it unto the seven churches** which are in Asia.

> **Revelation 22:16** – I Jesus have sent mine angel **to testify unto you these things in the churches.**

Clearly, the Apocalypse and all of its contents are consistently and exclusively addressed to the Church. It is a personal love letter from a Groom to his Bride. No other recipient is ever mentioned or even implied. The Church—and she alone—holds title to the entire Apocalypse.

Therefore, the 666 equation cannot be intended for post-Rapture believers or for any other group. It must be intended for the Bride of Christ. And that means the Church *today* is the entity that's expected to break the 666 code. In fact, that is precisely what John tells us to do. (See next item.)

 # 16. John commands the Church to decipher the 666 code.

In the thirteenth chapter of Revelation, John makes a statement that indisputably proves the Church might be able to discover the identity of the Beast: he *orders* the brethren to solve the 666 code!

Please read the verse below and think about what John is saying:

> **Revelation 13:18** (HCSB) – Here is wisdom: The one who has understanding **must calculate** the number of the beast, because it is the number of a man. His number is 666.

Look at that statement carefully. That's a command. John says to his audience, *You **must calculate** the number of the Beast!* And since John's audience is the Church—he repeatedly addresses the Book of Revelation to the brethren, and to no one else—then that command is *of necessity* directed exclusively to the Body of Christ.

In fact, if you read that verse again, you'll see that John is practically *shouting* the intended codebreaker is the Church because, according to him, solving this riddle requires "wisdom" and "understanding" — two attributes which God never ascribes to anyone but the Church:

> **Revelation 13:18** – Here is **wisdom**: The one who has **understanding** must calculate the number of the beast, because it is the number of a man. His number is 666.

> **Colossians 1:9** – We continually ask God to fill you [the Church] with...all the **wisdom** and **understanding** that the Spirit gives.

James 3:13 — Who is a **wise** man and endued with **knowledge** among you? let him shew out of a good conversation his works with meekness of **wisdom**. (Also see 2 Tim. 2:7, and Ps. 111:10.)

Hence, by calling on those with "wisdom" and "understanding" to solve this mystery, John is signaling *in no uncertain terms* it is the Church who is supposed to decipher it—not post-Rapture believers.

Now, I will admit that many people are going to study the book of Revelation after the Rapture and try to discover the Antichrist by using the 666 code. Some will even be "wise" enough to lead others to Christ by scouring the writings of today's prophecy experts (which will have been left behind on various bookshelves) and using that material to bring "understanding" about what is happening at that time (Dan. 12:3, 10).

But here is the catch: people who enter the Tribulation will have little time to solve one of the most difficult riddles ever recorded, namely, the number of the Beast recorded in Revelation 13:18. And second, even if people do solve it, what good will it do them? They will still have to remain on the earth and endure God's twenty-one judgments, regardless of whether they discover the algorithm that converts a man's name into 666. (Plus, there will be many other ways to identify the Beast at that time without resorting to numerology. See next item.)

That is why John never says, or even hints, that this clue is intended for post-Rapture believers. Instead, he says it is meant for the Church— i.e., those who possesses *all the wisdom and understanding that the Spirit gives*—because believers *today* are the ones who can actually use that cipher to point lost souls to Christ and help them avoid the fury of God altogether. Indeed, Scripture encourages the Church to seek the kind of "wisdom" needed to break these mysteries:

James 1:5 – If any of **you** [members of the <u>Church</u>] **lack wisdom,** let him ask of God, that giveth to all men **liberally**, and upbraideth not; and **it shall be given him.**

That's about as plain as it gets. When the Church asks God for wisdom —including the kind of "wisdom" that John says is needed to solve the 666 code—God gives us that wisdom. He gives it to us "liberally." James the apostle says so.

Therefore, assigning this cryptogram to anyone but the Church is to go beyond the plain meaning of the text, and past the numerous declarations that every part of Revelation is intended exclusively for the Body of Christ. Indeed, it is the Church—not post-Rapture believers—who absolutely need that clue. (See next item.)

17. The 666 code is a *pre-Tribulation* key to the Antichrist's identity.

Here is a startling fact: After the Rapture, the 666 code will *not* be needed to identify the Antichrist. The code must therefore be intended for believers who are present on earth *today*. In other words, it must be intended for *the Church*.

Let me say it again: The 666 code will not be needed to confirm the Antichrist's identity after the Rapture. Instead, it will be surprisingly easy to identify the Antichrist without resorting to numerology during the time of Jacob's Trouble. Why? Because the Antichrist will fulfill all of the *other* prophecies about him at that time, prophecies which are more than sufficient (in terms of number and detail) to locate him. The 666 code must therefore be intended for pre-Rapture believers. It must be intended for a group of people who have no other way to positively identify that man.

Think about that for a moment. Those who enter the Tribulation will *not* require the 666 code to identify Lucifer's son. Instead, the Man of Lawlessness will vividly *demonstrate* who he is by carrying out his most well-known and hideous exploits in front of the whole world. Tragically, those who remain after the Rapture will have more than enough indicators to recognize the Man of Sin *without* the 666 code.

People at that time will see a person who:

- Dupes Israel into a 7-year treaty of peace (Dan. 9:27)

- Takes control of a 10-nation military alliance in Europe (Rev. 17:12-13)

- Slays the Two Witnesses in the streets of Jerusalem (Rev. 11:7)

- Comes back to life after receiving a mortal wound (Rev. 13:3)

- Proclaims himself God in the rebuilt Temple (2 Thess. 2:4)

- Decapitates anyone who refuses the 666 mark (Rev. 13:15-17)

It won't take a great deal of spiritual insight to recognize the Antichrist then. And it certainly won't take an understanding of how his name adds to 666. Instead, anyone who enters the Tribulation with access to social media and all the above verses will be able to identify the Antichrist by simple comparison (provided they want to know the truth.)

Indeed, as if all these indicators weren't enough, the **Two Witnesses of Revelation 11** and the **Angel of Revelation 14:9** will actually point him out. These three individuals will say to the world, in effect, *There is the Beast! He is the spawn of Satan. Anyone who follows him or takes his mark will be doomed!*

> **Revelation 11:3, 7, 11, 12** – And I will give power unto my two witnesses, and they shall prophesy a thousand two hundred and threescore days, clothed in sackcloth... **And when they shall have finished their testimony, the beast that ascendeth out of the bottomless pit [i.e., the Antichrist] shall make war against them, and kill them**... And after three days and an half the spirit of life from God entered into them, and they stood upon their

feet; and great fear fell upon them which saw them. And they heard a great voice from heaven saying unto them, Come up hither. And they ascended up to heaven in a cloud; and their enemies beheld them.

Revelation 14:9, 10 – And the third angel followed them, saying with a loud voice, **If any man worship the beast [the Antichrist] and his image, and receive his mark in his forehead, or in his hand, the same shall drink of the wine of the wrath of God,** which is poured out without mixture into the cup of his indignation; and he shall be tormented with fire and brimstone in the presence of the holy angels, and in the presence of the Lamb.

Consequently, neither numerology nor code-breaking skills will be required by post-Rapture believers to locate the Antichrist once the Tribulation begins. Instead, his identity will be perfectly clear to anyone who is willing to compare him with Scripture, or at least pay attention to what the Angel and the Two Witnesses say.

On the other hand, we Christians who exist before the Rapture do not have the benefit of special angels or witnesses. Nor will the Antichrist draw attention to himself at the present time by committing open acts of violence. (Remember, according to Daniel 8:25, he rises on a platform of peace.)

Therefore, believers who inhabit the earth today need a different kind of clue. Something that is highly unique and objective. Something like the alpha-numeric sequence that God has provided in Revelation 13:18. Something like the number 666. With the 666 code, any person whom the Church suspects is the Antichrist can be quickly verified or disproved. But without that code, no confirmation today could be possible.

The 666 equation is therefore a pre-Tribulation key. It can be used right now to make a positive identification, but once the church leaves the earth and the Antichrist steps forward, that equation becomes almost pointless (in terms of its practical use in identifying the Antichrist.) I therefore believe that the Church, whom John *commanded* to count the number (Revelation 13:18), and to whom Jesus promised "**all truth**" concerning "**things to come**" (John 16:13), is the candidate most likely to receive the solution. We're the ones who need that clue.

18. Jesus commands the Church to study all of Revelation before he returns.

Lest any doubt remains that God expects his people to make a bona fide effort to break the 666 code, the Lord's threefold command to *the Church* to decipher the entire Apocalypse *before* he comes at the Rapture should settle the matter:

> **Revelation 1:3** – Blessed is he that...keep those things which are written therein: for the time is at hand.

> **Revelation 22:7** – Behold, I come quickly: blessed is he that keepeth the sayings of the prophecy of this book.

> **Revelation 22:10** – Seal not the sayings of the prophecy of this book: for the time is at hand.

Remember, Revelation is repeatedly addressed to the Church:

> **Revelation 1:11** – What thou seest, write in a book, and send it unto **the seven churches** which are in Asia.

> **Revelation 1:4** – John to **the seven churches** which are in Asia.

> **Revelation 22:16** – I Jesus have sent mine angel to testify unto you these things in **the churches.**

So, I ask you: What else does God have to say to prove he expects *the Church* to break the 666 code. How many more times does the Lord have to say it?

The fact is, God himself has commanded his people to decipher *all* the mysteries of the Apocalypse. And that includes every detail about the Antichrist—*including the 666 equation*—because all of that data is a part of those "things which are written therein." It is all in that "book." And no exclusions are listed.

In fact, just to make sure we don't miss the importance that God has attached to these particular mysteries, he commands us not once, but *three times* to thoroughly analyze the prophecies of the Apocalypse (the three verses cited above: Revelation 1:3, 22:7, 22:10). This is significant because, in Scripture, whenever God says something three times, he's telling us that "something" is extremely important. He's telling us we had better pay attention. And we had better do whatever the Lord requires thereby.

And just in case there is still any skepticism, note that these mysteries are to be deciphered before Jesus "comes quickly," which means *before Jesus returns at the Rapture.* How do we know that's what this phrase means? Because the Rapture is the only time when Jesus will come "quickly" or "unexpectedly."[16] It is the only event where Jesus' sudden arrival will bring a measure of protection and honor for those who have studied the Apocalypse:

> **Revelation 16:15** – Behold, I come as a thief. **Blessed** is he that **watcheth**, and keepeth his garments, lest he walk naked, and they see his shame.

Hence, it is the Church-age believers who are expected to break the 666 code, not post-Rapture saints.

---

[16] The phrase, "I come quickly," is acknowledged by many experts to be a synonym for the Rapture due to its context, which indicates a sudden, unexpected appearance.

* * * *

In short, when all of the evidence is put together, and we use common sense to correlate it, only one conclusion is possible: Jesus wants the Church to make a bona fide effort to locate the Man of Sin. If we are faithful in this regard and ask the Lord to explain his prophecies for us, then nothing in Revelation will remain "sealed." Not even the identity of the Antichrist.

Jesus says so.

Chapter 4

SUMMARY

SECTION I – *SCRIPTURE DOES NOT PROHIBIT THE CHURCH FROM RESEARCHING OR LEARNING THE IDENTITY OF THE ANTICHRIST*

1. Second Thessalonians does not say the Antichrist will suddenly be *identified* once the Restrainer is removed. It says he will suddenly be *unleashed* so that he can come to power and begin his campaign of death, destruction, and blasphemy.

2. The Bible never says: "It is *impossible* for the Church discover the identity of the Antichrist." Nor does it say: "The Church *must not look* for the Antichrist."

3. The Bible never says: "The Church cannot learn the identity of the Antichrist *until after* the Rapture (or the Abomination of Desolation, or the Seventh Trumpet, or Armageddon, or any other event.)"

4. The Bible never says: "God has hidden the identity of the Antichrist so well, *not even Satan* can know it."

5. The doctrine of imminence does not prevent knowing who the Antichrist is today. If the Antichrist was discovered right now, the date of the Rapture would *still be* unknown, and we'd still have to behave accordingly.

    Further, since the discovery of the Antichrist's identity is not a prerequisite to the Rapture—only a possibility—no contradiction exists between the doctrine of "imminence" (the notion that nothing has to occur before Jesus comes for the Church) and the discovery of the Antichrist.

6. The prohibition against knowing when the last days will start ended in 1948 with the rebirth of Israel. Therefore, for the last seventy years it has been the *duty* of the Church to recognize our proximity to the Rapture by looking for *all* of the signs that Jesus mentioned in the Olivet discourse, including the rise of false christs (Mt. 24:5).

7. Past failures to identify the Antichrist do not automatically negate the chance he may yet be identified.

SECTION II – *GOD SAVES PEOPLE BY REVEALING THE DETAILS OF PROPHECY*

8. God always warns his people that judgment is coming by telling them exactly what that judgment will be, and by giving them *signs* to prove that judgment is on the way.

9. God will not send any judgment until he has *first* unlocked at least some of his prophecies, so that people can be ready to make their escape. And sometimes the Lord even names *key individuals* in

those prophecies, so that his children will know when the critical moment has arrived!

10. God says it is an "honor" for us to solve his mysteries. The Lord therefore expects every believer to try and decipher the mysteries contained in his Word. And that includes riddles like the 666 code. In fact, it distresses the Lord when we fail to try!

SECTION III – *GOD WANTS THE CHURCH TO BREAK THE 666 CODE*

11. Common sense tells us that certain people in the enemy's camp *will know* who the Antichrist is well before the rest of the world does. Therefore, the identity of the Antichrist is not actually "unknowable" before the Rapture.

    Moreover, when we recall that God often mocks the enemy by divulging the enemy's secrets to faithful believers, it is entirely possible (if not actually probable) that God will divulge the identity of the Antichrist to the *Church* just before she's taken to heaven.

12. The existence of more than one hundred prophecies about the Antichrist implies that God expects us—the *Church*—to be familiar with those prophecies and to anticipate seeing their fulfillment in one particular person. All we have to do is ask.

13. Jesus promises to guide the *Church* into "all truth" concerning "things to come," i.e., things concerning the last days. And one of the greatest "truths" of the last days is the identity of the Antichrist.

14. The identity of the Antichrist is presented to the Church as a *riddle*—and riddles are always meant to be solved by the recipient.

15. The entire contents of Revelation, including the 666 code, are *addressed exclusively* to the Church. No other recipient—and thus no other code-breaker—is ever mentioned or even implied.

16. John *commands* his audience to break the 666 code. And we know his audience is the Church because that is to whom John addresses the Apocalypse. Moreover, only the Church has the "wisdom" and "understanding" which John says are needed to break the code.

17. The 666 code is a pre-Rapture key to the Antichrist's identity. It can be used to establish the Antichrist's identity today, but those who remain after the Rapture will be able to identify the Beast without the 666 code. The code is therefore intended for the *Church*, that is, people who actually need that clue in order to make an identification.

18. Jesus commands his Bride to study all the mysteries of Revelation—which necessarily includes the 666 code—*before* he returns at the Rapture. Therefore, the *Church* must be the intended "code-breaker" of the 666 riddle, not post-Rapture believers.

    Furthermore, no topic in the Apocalypse has been declared off-limits to the Church (except the words uttered by the Seven Thunders.) Indeed, Jesus promises to unseal all the mysteries of Revelation, provided we are faithful to study them.

Before closing this essay, permit me to say it one more time: No verse in Scripture requires the discovery of the Antichrist before the Rapture. But at the same time, when we consider all the evidence presented in this book, it is difficult to see how an identification prior to the Rapture could not occur.

In my opinion, the revelation of the Antichrist's identity simply depends on our willingness to study the Scriptures and to ask God's enlightenment. It is a *conditional* revelation. It is not required to be fulfilled prior to the Rapture, but it is a definite possibility, provided we all do our part.

* * * *

8 TIMES GOD PROMISES TO
UNSEAL END TIME PROPHECY

The following verses are reprinted to remind us that God will unseal the mysteries of the Apocalypse, the closer we get to the end. Each of the statements below *specifically* pertains to the unveiling of end-time events. (NKJV quoted.)

1. **Jeremiah 23:20** – The anger of the Lord will not turn back until He has executed and performed the thoughts of His heart. In the latter days you will understand it perfectly.

2. **Jeremiah 33:3** – Call to me, and I will answer you, and show you great and mighty things, which you do not know.

3. **Daniel 12:9-10** – The words are closed up and sealed till the time of the end... none of the wicked shall understand, but the wise shall understand.

4. **Amos 3:7** – Surely the Lord does nothing, unless He reveals His secret to His servants the prophets.

5. **Matthew 24:33** – When you see all these things, know that it is near—at the doors!

6. **John 16:13** – He [the Holy Spirit] will guide you into all truth ...and He will tell you things to come.

7. **Revelation 13:18** – Let him who has understanding calculate the number of the Beast, for it is the number of a man: His number is 666.

8. **Revelation 22:10** – Do not seal the words of the prophecy of this book, for the time is at hand.

* * * *

**Please see Appendix B for additional evidence
that the Antichrist can be identified today.**

Chapter 5

HOW TO IDENTIFY THE ANTICHRIST

AS I MENTIONED EARLIER, God has provided all the tools necessary for the Church to identify the Man of Sin today. Those tools come in the form of more than a dozen unique prophecies that will manifest in the Antichrist *before* he comes to power.

Therefore, since we have now established that it might be possible to identify the Antichrist today, the Church (in my view) has a duty to monitor prominent international leaders, and then use the clues in Scripture to evaluate any person whom she suspects is the Beast of the Apocalypse. The only condition is that we approach this research with respect and humility. We must conduct it in a manner that is both fitting and pleasing to God (1 Cor. 14:40). Sensationalism and wild speculation are out; prayerful analysis and sober discussion are in. The fate of thousands of souls might hang in the balance.

To begin this search for the Beast, seven clues are provided below as a quick review. A **full explanation** of these clues (and many others) are covered in my book, ***Empire of the Antichrist***.

APPEARANCE

▶ **The Antichrist will look like Augustus, Tiberius, Caligula, Claudius, or Nero:**

- Rev. 17:10-11 – He is "[one] of the seven" Caesars of ancient Rome.

- Rev. 17:8 – People shall "wonder" at this Caesar's return.

NATIONALITY

► **The Antichrist will be an Italian**:

- Gen. 3:15 – The final empire of prophecy is Rome.
- Dan. 9:26 – The Antichrist is a prince of the Romans.
- Ex. 21:25 – Divine retribution requires that an Italian Caesar be punished for the execution of Jesus.
- Rev. 17:9-11 – The Antichrist completes a line of eight Italian Caesars.

NAME

► **The Antichrist's name will add to 666**:

- Rev. 13:18 – When properly spelled in Greek or Hebrew, and assigned the correct numeric values, the letters in the Antichrist's name will total 666.

RELIGION

► **The Antichrist will be a Roman Catholic**:

- Rev. 17:3-6 – The Whore "sits" on the Beast.
  - The Beast in this scene is the Antichrist "spirit."
  - The Whore is the "city of seven hills," Rome (v. 17:9, 18).

  Hence, from God's point of view, the city of Rome is ensconced on the spirit of Antichrist. And since the religion of Rome is Roman Catholicism, then the Antichrist himself must be a Roman Catholic.

PROFESSION

► **The Antichrist will be a professional peacemaker**:

- Dan. 9:27 – He will "confirm the covenant" between the people of Israel, the Arabs, and the international community.

GOAL

▶ **The Antichrist will advocate world government**:

  ▪ Rev. 13:7 – He will be given "power…over all kindreds, and tongues, and nations."

ANTI-SEMITISM

▶ **The Antichrist will hate faithful Jews and Christians**:

  ▪ Dan. 8:24 – He will "destroy the mighty and the holy people."

Using these prophecies—and at least five or six more—the Church can easily determine whether a given general, bureaucrat, businessman, or religious leader is the Antichrist.

Remember, Jesus *commands us* to be aware of false christs (along with other prophetic developments) so that we won't be deceived by the enemy and miss the Rapture (Mt. 24:4-5; Lk. 21:36; Mt. 25:1-13).

The following chart can help initiate our search for the enemy by *eliminating* a number of popular candidates at the outset. Upon seeing that none of these men actually meet the biblical qualifications, we can then direct our time and energy towards other, lesser-known leaders and kingpins:

Antichrist Candidate Chart

Name	Italian	Catholic	Name adds to 666	Caesar Look-alike	Peace Maker	World Gov't	Anti-Israel
Yuval Noah Harari (WEF speaker)						✓	
Klaus Schwab (WEF Chairman)						✓	
Emmanuel Macron (France)			(✓)		✓	✓	
Barack Obama			(✓)			✓	✓
Pope Francis†		✓	(✓)			✓	✓
King Charles III (UK)			(✓)		✓	✓	
King Juan Carlos (Spain)		✓	(✓)			✓	
Donald Trump			(✓)				
Jared Kushner					✓		
Bill Gates						✓	
Elon Musk							
Ayatollah Khamenei (Iran)						✓	✓
Recep Erdogan (Turkey)			(✓)			✓	✓
Javier Solana (WEU Chief)			(✓)		✓	✓	
Bill Clinton					✓	✓	
Vladimir Putin							✓
True Antichrist	✓	✓	✓	✓	✓	✓	✓

(✓) – Calculations were necessarily "creative." The 666 value is therefore in doubt.

† – Pope Francis has Italian parents, but he was born in Buenos Aires. By contrast, the Antichrist will have Italian parents *and* he will be born in Italy, to fully validate his Roman heritage.

As you can see, none of today's most popular candidates matches all of these characteristics. No one even comes close. But a person is coming in the not-too-distant future who will meet every qualification. And, as Pastor Breese has said, if the Church is alert and uses the tools that God has provided, it may be possible for the Church to spot that person. Should that happen, we will then know the Rapture is near, "even at the doors."

Chapter 6

NONE SO BLIND

THERE'S AN OLD ADAGE which says there are none so blind as those who will not see. Unfortunately, people of all religious backgrounds today—*including many Christians!*—are proving that adage once again. How? By willfully ignoring the signs that confirm our planet is about to embark on a seven-year nightmare known as the Tribulation.

With few exceptions, the vast majority of men and women today absolutely refuse to recognize the unprecedented events, natural disasters, and alignment of nations which the Bible says will precede that terrible epoch. Indeed, one of the most common refrains I hear from people concerning the Rapture and the Tribulation goes something like this:

> *I know that wars and famines are supposed to foretell the end of the age, but we've always had wars and famines! There have always been earthquakes and "signs in the sky"! Christians have always claimed that Armageddon was right around the corner! But their doom and gloom predictions never came true. So why should we believe that kind of sensationalism now?*

To a certain extent, I can understand why many people feel this way. Ever since Jesus ascended back to heaven in 32 A.D., there have been wars and famines, along with earthquakes, comets, storms, and locusts. And right behind those, there have been prophets and preachers claiming that doomsday was nigh.

A well-visited Wikipedia page reports that over the last two millennia not less than 170 claims have been made predicting the end of the world. Yet all of those claims were wrong.

But here's the twist: This time around things are different. Drastically different. They're different because for the first time in history over two dozen prophecies—both unprecedented and highly specific—have appeared on the scene. And all of them are converging like laser beams trained on the head of a firing pin.

Indeed, our generation—and only our generation—is the first to see the creation or rise of such things as:

- Weapons of Mass Destruction (Rev. 8:7-12 with Mt. 24:22)

- An ecumenical movement led by Rome (Rev. 13:4 with 17:1-2)

- Electronic monetary systems and bio-chips (Rev. 13:16-17)[17]

- Nations able to field armies of 200 million men (Rev. 9:13-19)[18]

- A world government in-waiting—the United Nations (Rev. 13:7)

- A new Roman Empire in the form of the EI2 (Rev. 17:12-14)

- An imminent peace treaty between Israel and her Arab neighbors (Dan. 9:27)[19]

---

[17] For example, several major retailers are now working with credit card companies to create a device that will control all sales by means of a "hand scan." See https://www.cnbc.com/2020 /01/18/amazon-reportedly-wants-to-turn-your-hand-into-a-credit-card.html

[18] The combined military forces of East Asian nations—China, Japan, North and South Korea, India, Indonesia, Malaysia, etc.—now total about 5 million men. However, given a sufficiently desperate conflict, such as a regional campaign by China to subjugate the entire East Asian theater, the number of people directly involved in the fighting could easily swell to 200 million, especially if the fighting descends into urban warfare.

[19] The imminence of this treaty was confirmed in a speech that was given by Israeli Prime Minister Benjamin Netanyahu on 9/22/2016 at the United Nations. Please see the YouTube video at https://www.youtube.com/watch?v=WmRQE7QSA00&t=1936s [4:00 - 17:30]

- The completion of preparations for the Temple's reconstruction (Dan. 9:27)[20]

- The sanctioning of full-term abortion by many countries (Mk. 9:42)

- A steep rise in the total number of natural disasters, such as earthquakes, floods, hurricanes, volcanic eruptions, and weather anomalies (Mt. 24:7)[21]

- An explosion of UFO sightings and ET encounters (Lk. 21:11, 25)[22]

- Rampant apostasy in the Church, including such false doctrines as hyper-grace, emergent church, Theosophy, same-sex marriage, female pastorship, "reconciliation" with Rome, etc. (1 Tim. 4; Acts 20:28-30; 2 Peter 2:6)

In my opinion, one would have to be willfully blind to look at these unparalleled events and *not* see what the Bible predicts. A person would have to be covering his face with both hands *not* to see that all of these developments are without precedent, that they're converging at the same moment in history, and that they were predicted in the Bible.

Again, the problem isn't a lack of signs. It's the refusal of men and women to accept the signs and admit what they mean. It is nothing less than a conscious decision to be willfully ignorant.

---

[20] The Temple Institute in Jerusalem has already created all of the architectural drawings, implements, and supplies needed to build the Temple and carry out the rituals. The Aaronic priesthood has been genetically identified, the priests have been trained, and a red heifer (the ashes of which are needed to purify the altar) is today being raised in a secret location. See, for example: https://www.breakingisraelnews.com/123800/imminent-return-red-heifer-fact-fiction

[21] See, for example, The Economist article at: https://www.economist.com/graphic-detail/2017/08/29/weather-related-disasters-are-increasing

[22] Since 1947, when the modern UFO era officially began, the number of UFO encounters has skyrocketed. See, for example, the Wikipedia article at: https://en.wikipedia.org/wiki/List_of_reported_UFO_sightings

The apostle Peter described this "see-no-evil" attitude that people would exhibit at the end of the age:

> **2 Peter 3:3-7** (NKJV) – [K]nowing this first: that scoffers will come in the last days, **walking according to their own lusts**, and saying, "Where is the promise of His coming? For since the fathers fell asleep, all things continue as *they were* from the beginning of creation." For this **they willfully forget: that by the word of God** the heavens were of old, and the earth standing out of water and in the water, by which **the world *that* then existed perished, being flooded with water**. But the heavens and the earth *which* are now preserved by the same word, are reserved for fire until the day of judgment and perdition of ungodly men.

Notice that Peter zeroes in on the defiant attitude of men and women just before Jesus returns. People will be so deep in their lust and rebellion, he says, they will actually mock those who claim that Judgment is near, even though the proof is staring them right in the face!

People will ignore that proof, says Peter, and even deny that a similar judgment took place during the Flood because their hearts will be so hard. And, if they won't accept the reality of a historical event for which there is overwhelming data,[23] then they'll never accept the evidence for a judgment that lies in the future.

Men and women will be so spiritually dense, says Peter, they will deny both historian and prophet. They will mock the idea of a looming

---

[23] According to Peter, people will deny that the Flood of Noah ever took place, despite all the evidence that it did. This includes such facts as: the existence of virtually identical Flood stories among dozens of disparate cultures, common DNA markers that tie all humans to a genetic Adam and Eve, historical migration patterns that emanate from Mesopotamia (Shinar), and the geologic record, including such things as vast graveyards of suddenly buried animals and flora (in places all over the world), sea creature fossils embedded in mountain tops, rapidly formed sediment layers on every continent, and trees (and other perishable objects) that vertically penetrate these (supposedly millions of years old) layers.

Judgment, and refuse to repent, even after they see such things as: the rise of a world government (Rev. 13:7), the return of the Roman Empire (Rev. 17:12), a move towards religious unity (Rev. 13:8), instantaneous telecommunications (Mt. 24:15; Rev. 11:9), weapons of mass destruction (Mt. 24:22), the rebirth of the nation of Israel (Ez. 37; Mt. 24:32), and so on.

CONCLUSION

The sad truth is that our world is on the fast track to Judgment, and mankind is now split into two groups.

The first group consists of those whom the Bible calls *wise* (Mt. 24:45). These are the people who rejoice at the thought of taking part in the Rapture and meeting their Lord face-to-face at any moment. Their primary concern is to please God and to bring in the lost. Their utmost desire is to be counted worthy to escape all those things that are coming upon the earth and to stand before the Son of Man.

This group will continue to grow in spiritual wisdom and personal righteousness. These are the Christians who've read the Good Book and see all the signs foretold by Daniel, Jesus, and John. They strive to live pure lives and make the best use of the remaining time.

The second group, on the other hand, consists of those whom the Bible calls *wicked* (Mt. 24:48). These individuals will never see the signs because they refuse to see them. In fact, they don't even care about the signs or how close we are to Jesus' return. (And many such people are a part of the Church!) Despite all the unparalleled events and developments that have emerged in the last seven decades, this group will only continue to grow more sinful and deviant. They will only continue to walk "according to their own lusts."

Even with all the alarms going off in their consciences, they will not repent of their sins or give glory to God. Instead, just like the people of Noah's day, they will wait until the "door of the Ark" has been shut and the judgments begin to fall. Only then, it will be too late.[24]

I pray, therefore, that all of us will renew our determination to seek God's face, carry our cross, and lead others to Christ. Now is the time to reach our neighbors. We must bring them the Good News before it's too late.

---

[24] During the Tribulation people still can be saved from eternal damnation, but tragically, they will have to endure the horrors of the Tribulation until they perish or Jesus returns.

Chapter 7

HELL IS FOR REAL

ACCORDING TO A RECENT SURVEY conducted by the Pew Research Center[25], less than 60% of Americans believe in a literal hell. In Western Europe, that number is even lower. But the Bible is clear— hell is for real. And it's the most horrible place one could imagine.

The Old Testament describes hell as a place of:

> ➢ Everlasting shame (Dan. 12:2)

> ➢ Eternal fire (Deut. 32:22; Is. 66:24)

> ➢ No hope for redemption (Job 7:9-10)

> ➢ Unending anguish (Ps. 116:3)

Later on, in the New Testament, Jesus also spoke about hell. In fact, he spoke about hell more than anyone else in the entire Bible. Jesus said that hell was originally prepared for the devil and his angels (Mt. 25:41). It was created to punish Satan for his wanton rebellion, and for his attempt to usurp God's throne (Is. 14:12-14).

Indeed, Jesus' descriptions of hell are the most detailed and sobering in all of Scripture. Jesus described hell as a place where people:

---

[25] https://www.pewresearch.org/fact-tank/2015/11/10/most-americans-believe-in-heaven-and-hell

- Are continually tormented by their memories (Lk. 16:25)

- Suffer unending heat and flames (Mt. 13:41-42, 49-50)

- Endure unquenchable thirst (Lk. 16:24)

- Are covered in horrible maggots (Mk. 9:48)

- Desperately wish to go back and warn their loved ones of the horrors that await all those who refuse to put away sin and follow the Lord (Lk. 16:27-28)

Tragically, the vast majority of mankind is on its way to this inferno. Jesus said in Matthew 7:13-14:

> Enter ye in at the strait gate: for **wide is the gate**, and **broad is the way**, that leadeth to destruction, and **many there be** which go in thereat: Because strait is the gate, and narrow is the way, which leadeth unto life, and **few there be that find it**.

And that's not all. Even many people who call themselves "Christian" are going to have a rude awakening on the Day of Judgment. According to Matthew 7:21-23:

> Not every one that saith unto me, Lord, Lord, shall enter into the kingdom of heaven; but he that doeth the will of my Father which is in heaven. Many will say to me in that day, Lord, Lord, have we not prophesied in thy name? and in thy name have cast out devils? and in thy name done many wonderful works? And then will I profess unto them, **I never knew you**: depart from me, ye that work iniquity.

How tragic! My heart literally breaks at the thought of so many people finding out they are not going to make it.

In view of these statements, the question arises, How could a loving God send millions of people to a place of such unspeakable torment? How could Jesus condemn most of humanity to suffer the ravages of hell for all eternity?

The answer is because all men and women—including this author—have broken God's Law. We have crossed the Ten Commandments. All of us, at one time or another, have either lied, stolen, coveted, committed sexual sin, dishonored God, or dishonored our parents. We are therefore deserving of God's wrath.

That might sound like a harsh pronouncement to some, especially since Scripture repeatedly says that God is "good." But it is God's goodness that requires him to punish all evildoers. In the same way that a "good" judge must punish a murderer or rapist, God's goodness requires that he punish all thieves, liars, blasphemers, and adulterers. If God did not punish such people, he would no longer be "good."

But here's the great news: God doesn't want to do that! Instead, God is so rich in mercy that he's made a way of escape. That "way" is both simple and free. It's available to every person on earth. And it satisfies the requirements of God's perfect justice. In fact, the moment any person chooses that path, that person is instantly taken off "death row," declared "not guilty," and welcomed by God as a friend. The "way" of which I speak, of course, is Jesus of Nazareth—the Way, the Truth, and the Life (John 14:6).

As you may have heard, about two thousand years ago, God dealt with man's sin by sending his only begotten son to take the punishment that you and I deserve. Jesus sacrificed his life on the Cross, so that you and I don't have to "sacrifice" our lives in hell. Jesus' crucifixion satisfies the requirements of the Law and legally pays the entire fine, so that you and I can go free.

As a result, the moment we repent (make a conscious decision that we no longer want to serve sin) and put our faith in Christ (decide that we want to serve the Lord), God will transfer Jesus' perfect righteousness to our account and drop all the charges against us. He will declare us "not guilty," and throw our case out of court. At that very instant, he will change our eternal destiny from one of everlasting anguish, suffering, and torment, to one of unending peace, joy, love, and fulfillment.

Indeed, the rewards that await those who genuinely love God are beyond description. As the Scriptures say:

> **I Corinthians 2:9** – Eye hath not seen, nor ear heard, neither have entered into the heart of man, the things which God hath prepared for them that love him.

My fervent prayer is that you, too, will choose to love God and receive his eternal blessings, through Jesus, his son. I pray you will do this today.

AFTERWORD

ALLOW ME to express my deepest gratitude to the Lord for my salvation and for his multiplied blessings. His guidance and support throughout this project have been utterly amazing—and quite humbling.

I would also like to thank the innumerable pastors, scholars, and authors who have laid the groundwork for me, by providing laymen (such as myself) with access to their research and conclusions through such media as books, videos, and live sermons. Your works are precious.

To the reader, thank you for taking the time to consider this short collection of thoughts. I hope it will bless you and help you draw closer to Christ.

As stated previously, please understand this book assumes the reader has a good handle on the basics of Bible prophecy. *God Says Count the Number 666!* is meant to answer a particular question, namely, whether or not it's possible for the Church to learn the identity of the Antichrist before the Rapture. This book is not meant as an overview of the end times. Nevertheless, I have tried to guide the reader (where appropriate) by clarifying how the possibility of discovering the Antichrist's identity fits within the overall prophetic tapestry.

With these thoughts in mind, permit me to briefly state my approach to the chronology of Bible prophecy:

Futurist - The vast majority of the events of Revelation 4-22, are still future. They were not fulfilled during the Jewish Rebellion in 70 A.D., nor are they a mere allegory of the struggle between good and evil.

Pre-Tribulational - The Rapture will take place before the Tribulation begins. Christ will come for his Church and take her to heaven before the start of Daniel's 70th Week (before the treaty of Daniel 9:27 is signed.)

Pre-Millennial - Christ will return physically to the earth prior to the start of his one-thousand-year reign from Jerusalem.

Dispensational - Throughout history, men have always been justified by turning from sin (repenting) and obeying God's commands (exhibiting faith). But God has divided history into seven epochs, or dispensations, specifying, in each, how people are to express their faith at that moment. These epochs include: Innocence, Conscience, Government, Promise, Law, Grace, and The Kingdom. Currently, we're in the dispensation of Grace.

Additionally, as we go through this study we should always remember that the hero of prophecy is Jesus of Nazareth. He alone is the one who redeems mankind from eternal destruction. He is therefore the focus and fulfillment of God's prophetic Word:

Christ-centered - The Bible repeatedly declares that Jesus Christ is the center and fullness of prophecy. Consequently, the prophetic Word always pivots on one of two things: Jesus' First Advent and the Cross, or Jesus' Second Advent and Armageddon (and, by extension, the Millennial Kingdom.) Of all the concepts that guide our study of eschatology, this is by far the most important. Prophecy centers on Christ:

> **John 5:39** (NKJV) - You search the Scriptures, for in them you think you have eternal life; and these are they which testify of Me.

> **Acts 3:20-21** - And he shall send Jesus Christ...which God hath spoken by the mouth of all His holy prophets since the world began.

Jewish Context - Immediately beneath that is a corollary: Bible prophecy always takes place within the context of Israel. Without the

Jews, there are no prophets, there is no Bible, and we have no Messiah. Indeed, it is because of the Jewish people's willingness to endure untold suffering and sorrow—for centuries—that we have a chance to escape the Judgment. As the apostle John once said, "[S]alvation is of the Jews" (Jn. 4:22). For these reasons, the land and people of Israel will always be at the center of Bible prophecy. They are God's special children, and neither the Church nor anyone else will replace them.

Accordingly, eschatology always focuses on, and unfolds within, the geography, culture, events, politics, miracles, and people of Israel:

> **Romans 9:3-5** - [M]y countrymen according to the flesh,
> who are Israelites, to whom pertain the adoption, the glory,
> the covenants, the giving of the law, the service of God,
> and the promises.

The impact of the above two principles is this: Every major prophecy of Scripture is tethered to the person of Jesus Christ and his mission to save mankind—especially his mission to save the nation of Israel. Therefore, any analysis which fails to include or acknowledge this crucial aspect of the prophetic Word is inherently flawed.

* * * *

Finally, it might be helpful to review the "Rules of Interpretation" section, contained in Appendix A. These are ten basic guidelines that will help keep us on track with the various prophecies and associated narratives. Whenever the discussion requires it, the appropriate rule will be cited so you can follow my reasoning (e.g., "Rule 2"). The section is pretty short and I think you'll find it both fascinating and informative.

* * * *

P.S. – You'll notice I quote from a number of different Bible versions throughout this essay. Some might question this practice, but I wanted to make sure that, in every case, the intent of the original words was expressed as closely as possible. Unfortunately, in English, there is no version of Scripture which is always accurate. Some versions add words, others delete words, and some even change words. I therefore make it a point to use the version which, I believe, most closely reflects the original Hebrew and Greek, and which preserves the essential meaning of the verse I am quoting. My goal is to be accurate.

* * * * *

Dear Reader,

If you enjoyed this book, it would mean a lot to this author if you could leave a short review on Amazon or on any of your favorite bookstore websites. Your input would help me fine tune my upcoming essays, and it would give other last days enthusiasts a chance to gauge the quality of these works up front.

Thank you for taking an interest in Bible prophecy and for giving me an opportunity to share some of my thoughts and insights with you. Writing this book has been a blessing to me, and I hope that reading *God Says Count the Number 666!* has been a blessing to you, as well!

Sincerely,

Charles "Ken" Bassett

Email: ckbassett777@yahoo.com

* * * * *

APPENDIX A

RULES OF INTERPRETATION

EVERY SERIOUS RESEARCHER knows that to correlate and make sense of volumes of data, one must first establish some basic assumptions and rules of interpretation. That's because our rules and assumptions provide the logical framework on which to hang our data and build reasonable theories and conclusions.

This is true regardless of whether one is engaged in archaeology, astrophysics, crime scene analysis, or Bible prophecy. Our rules of interpretation dictate whether we will solve the puzzle or keep running in circles.

I have therefore compiled a number of ground rules for this study and placed them below. I think most expositors will agree they're both useful and reasonable, because students of prophecy have been applying these guidelines for decades. The key is to apply them with discipline. If we truly wish to unlock the treasures that God has hidden in prophecy, we must stick to these rules as closely as possible.

Accordingly, whenever the discussion calls for it, the appropriate rule will be cited so you can follow my reasoning. I think you'll find this section both fascinating and informative.

1. When the plain sense makes sense, seek no other sense.

   o This axiom was coined by Dr. David L. Cooper of The Biblical Research Society in the early 1900s. The full hermeneutic reads: "**When the plain sense of Scripture makes common sense, seek no other sense**; therefore, take every word at its primary, ordinary, usual, literal meaning unless the facts of the immediate context, studied in the light of related passages and axiomatic and fundamental truths, indicate clearly otherwise."

o Allow me to translate the essence of this statement: When the narrative reads like a news report or an eyewitness account, then take it as a news report or an eyewitness account. When the text says "this is a parable," then take it as a parable and find out what each symbol stands for. (Usually, **the symbols will be explained right in the passage**. If not, they will be explained **somewhere else in Scripture**.)

When the narrative uses hyperbole, such as when a person says, "I'm so hungry I could eat a horse," or, "He's ten times smarter than me," then we know exaggerated language is being used to emphasize a point. We don't need to take the phrase literally. Likewise, when a prophet says he sees a sign or a vision—either on earth or in heaven—then we know that sign or vision stands for something real. Our job then is to determine what that "something" is from the **surrounding text**, or from a **relevant passage elsewhere in Scripture**.

2. There must be no *re*-interpretation of *the* interpretation.

o Once a symbol is explained in the text, that explanation cannot be re-interpreted by an expositor to mean something else. Otherwise, the authoritative definition (from God) is voided and we immediately depart into error. This may sound obvious enough, but many expositors ignore this critical guideline and then re-interpret the very definition provided in the passage. The resulting confusion has led to unrecoverable errors.

For example, even though Revelation 17 explicitly says the Seven Heads of the Beast represent seven kings, many expositors skirt that definition and then re-interpret the seven *kings* to mean seven *kingdoms*. This one error (by itself) is perhaps the single greatest impediment to solving the mysteries of the Apocalypse. **If an explicit definition is provided in the text, we must accept it "as is." Barring any**

**additional statements within the interpretation itself, we
must not change that interpretation or go beyond it:**

> **Deuteronomy 4:2** – Ye shall not add unto the word which
> I command you, neither shall ye diminish ought from it, that
> ye may keep the commandments of the Lord your God
> which I command you.

> [Also see Proverbs 30:5-6 and Revelation 22:18-19.]

3. Numbers carry both literal and symbolic meaning in prophecy.

    o   **The number 3** can literally refer to three items on a list (such
        as the Three Woes of Revelation 8.) But it can also indicate
        the **beginning, middle, and end of a set**. For example,
        Daniel's "seventy weeks" (in Daniel 9) certainly consist of
        seventy weeks (specifically, seventy weeks of years.) But the
        seventy are divided into three groups to indicate the
        beginning weeks (7), the middle weeks (62), and the final
        week (1). (Please see chart below.)

A CONSTRUCT OF 3 RELATED ITEMS INDICATES THE CHRONOLOGICAL BEGINNING, MIDDLE, AND END OF A SET

SET	BEGINNING	MIDDLE	END
Bible	Genesis ("Beginnings")	Exodus – Jude	Revelation (End of the Age)
Harvests of Israel[1]	First Fruits	Main Harvest	Gleanings
Restoration of Israel[2]	Bones	Flesh	Breath
The Book of Revelation[3]	Things already seen	Things that are	Things that shall be hereafter
70 Weeks of Daniel[4]	7 Weeks	62 Weeks	1 Week
Tribulation Judgements	Seals	Trumpets	Bowls
Caesars of Ancient Rome[5]	5 Fallen	1 Living	1 Coming

Notes: 1 - Ex. 23:16 and Lev. 19:9-10
2 - Ez. 37:7-10
3 - Rev. 1:19
4 - Dan. 9:24-27
5 - Rev. 17:10

o **The number 7** represents a **complete group or an entire set**. This is true even if that set has more than seven com-ponents. For example, the seven churches of Revelation are indeed seven literal churches. But they also stand for the complete set of churches that exist from the time of John to the Rapture. In other words, the seven churches of Revelation cover the entire church age. They effectively represent tens of thousands of congregations, over a 2000-year period.

4. God builds precept upon precept.

o God is not the author of confusion. Instead, he sets a pattern or an outline, and then adds all the details to that outline in a progressive manner. Line upon line, precept upon precept, until the entire picture has formed—**yet always in accordance with the original pattern** (Is. 28:10). Once the pattern or outline is set, **all subsequent outlines and data must align with the original scheme**. Why? Because there *must be* a fixed point of reference, a grand super-structure, in order to make sense of all the information. This is key.

Indeed, this principle is so foundational to the interpretation of God's Word that it's presented in the very first book of the Bible. There, in Genesis 37, we learn how God told Joseph through two separate dreams that his family would someday bow down to him. The symbols in each dream were *different* (sheaves vs. stars), but the message in each case was *identical* (your family will bow to your authority.) This principle is then repeated in Genesis 41 when God tells Pharaoh through two separate dreams that Egypt was about to experience seven years of plenty, followed by seven years of famine. The symbols in each dream were *different* (cows vs. corn stalks), but the message in each case was *identical* (store up your goods before the curse of God falls.)

Indeed, anyone who has sat in a classroom knows this is exactly how the best teachers keep their students on-track when conveying difficult concepts: establish an outline first, then add all the facts, concepts, and analogies—but always in accordance with the original outline. This is how the best teachers teach, and it's exactly how God develops the truths in His Word. Master outline, details, sub-outlines, repeat. If this principle was not in the DNA of God's prophetic Word, it would be impossible to connect the dots with any reliability. Confusion would reign...and God is not the author of confusion.

5. All the major details must be accounted for.

    o   There's no such thing as partial credit when it comes to interpreting prophecy. The interpretation is either all right, or it's all wrong. The details are either all accounted for, or they're all suspect. That's because the Word of God is logical, accurate, and complete in all respects…and thus **the "lens" or "prism" through which a prophetic passage is interpreted must produce a scenario that's logical, accurate, and complete in all respects**, as well. If an expositor's lens (that is, his interpretive filter or starting point through which the details are analyzed) can explain four components of a prophecy, but not the fifth, then something is wrong with that lens. Likewise, if an expositor ignores a major clue, or if he stretches the interpretation of that clue just to make it "fit" his theory, then his scenario is inherently flawed. It must be reevaluated and, if necessary, discarded.

    This is not to disparage any expositor or his work. All current interpretations of prophecy—including mine—stand on the accumulated knowledge, research, and hypotheses of thousands of incredibly gifted scholars and pastors who've come before. The point is simply that we must judge a scenario based on its cohesiveness and ability to explain all the major details. Otherwise, we'll never arrive at the right conclusions.

6. It's not rocket science.

    o   Inasmuch as Jesus commanded the humble churches in Asia Minor to study and decipher the prophecies of Revelation, we know that the correct interpretation of those prophecies must be relatively simple. **It shouldn't take a degree in theology or ancient history to explain the various symbols or to grasp their meaning**.

For instance, Jesus was able to explain *all* of the Old Testament prophecies which proved he was the Messiah in less than three hours, as he walked with two of his disciples on the road to Emmaus. (See Luke 24:13-35.)

Similarly, the people who made up the churches of Revelation were simple farmers, laborers, merchants, and craftsmen, not post-graduates of a theological seminary. (Although I'm very glad we have such seminaries!) The original seven congregations scattered around Asia Minor would have been familiar with the Roman emperors, their own national history, the local cults, and the Scriptures, but not much more.

Thus, any analysis that relies on a novel translation of the text, or cleverly nuanced scenarios, or long-winded essays, is probably wrong. The text of the Bible is clear and concise, and therefore the explanation of prophecy should be clear and concise, as well. The prophet Daniel, for example, said the interpretation of his prophecies would occur as a function of *time* and a person's *faith in God's Word*, not as a function of academic IQ. (Specifically, Daniel said his prophecies would be understood in the *last days* by those who were *spiritually wise*.)

Thus, as we attempt to unlock the mysteries of Daniel and John, a good rule of thumb is to look for the simplest answer that can account for all the details, while still adhering to the biblical text. We shouldn't have to go very far to find the solution.

[Again, this is not to detract from the inestimable work of those who've given us the foundations of modern eschatology. It is simply a way to gauge the validity of *any* interpretation—including mine—by acknowledging the fact that deciphering prophecy should be a relatively straight-forward proposition. All one needs is a working knowledge of God's Word (2 Tim. 2:15) and a genuine love for Christ (Jn. 16:13).]

7. Prophets look forward, not backward.

    o   Each of the narratives recorded by Daniel and John begins in
        the time-frame that exists at the moment the prophecy is
        given. The narratives then proceed from that point into the
        future; they never look back. This is because prophecy, by its
        very nature, is not concerned with the past, but with what will
        happen in the future if people refuse to put away sin and turn
        to God. The only exception to this rule is when the narrative
        requires a set-up, and then only briefly.

        Thus, Daniel 2 and 7 start their narratives with Babylon,
        because the Babylonian kings were firmly in power when
        Daniel received those visions. Daniel 8 starts with a
        description of the Medo-Persian Empire, because the Medes
        were getting ready to supplant Babylon when that vision was
        given. Similarly, Revelation 12 begins with the activities of
        the Roman Empire, because that was the empire in power
        when John received the Apocalypse.

8. There will be exactly four prophetic empires in history.

    The prophet Daniel taught in verses 2:40 and 7:17 that from the
    sixth century B.C. until the establishment of God's kingdom on
    earth, exactly **four empires** would rise on the timeline of
    prophecy:

        Daniel7:7 (GW) — Four kingdoms...will rise to power on
        the earth.

    In Daniel 2 these four empires are represented by the **four
    components** of a statue that appeared in a dream to King
    Nebuchadnezzar of Babylon. They included: a head of gold, arms
    of silver, a belly and thighs of brass, and legs of iron. (The legs of
    iron represent phase one of the final empire; the feet of iron and
    clay represent phase two of the same empire.)

The four prophetic empires appear again in Daniel 7. But in this case they are represented by **four vicious animals**: a winged lion, a lopsided bear, a four-headed leopard, and a strange beast with ten horns. (The beast itself represents phase one of the final empire; the horns of the beast represent phase two.)

In the New Testament, this same "empire count" is repeated. It's reflected in the **four components** of a terrifying beast that appears in Revelation 13. The four components include: the body of a leopard, the feet of a bear, the mouth of a lion, and the beast as a whole.

Although the Bible never says why these four empires *in particular* are included on the list, one can make an educated guess. Apparently, it's because all of them share two unique characteristics.

First, each of these empires—and only these empires— subjugated the sovereign nation of Judaea. And second, each of these empires—and only these empires—directly threatened the line of Messiah by concentrating their forces on the tribe of Judah, the line through which Jesus was to come, thus threatening the entire plan of Salvation.

Consequently, as we go forward and attempt to explain the symbology of Daniel and the Apocalypse, we must stay within the framework of **exactly four empires**—not five, or seven, or eight, as some suggest.

9. In the Apocalypse, one symbol can represent several entities.

    o Whereas the prophet Daniel uses several symbols to represent a single entity—for example, in referring to Greece he uses a torso of bronze (v. 2:32), a four-headed leopard (v. 7:6), and a goat with a large horn (v. 8:5)—**John the Revelator**

reverses that formula and uses one symbol to represent several entities.

For instance, in Revelation 12, the **Dragon** represents:

- The Antichrist spirit – Satan (Rev. 12:9)
- The Antichrist forces – An imperial army (Rev. 12:13-15)
- The Antichrist person – Seven kings (Rev. 12:3, 17:10)

In Revelation 13 and 17 the **Beast from the Sea** represents:

- The Antichrist spirit – Satan (Rev. 17:3)
- The Antichrist forces – An imperial army (Rev. 13:7)
- The Antichrist person – The Eighth King (Rev. 13:18)

In Revelation 17 and 18 the **Whore of Babylon** represents a certain city that is:

- A religious capital (Rev. 17:4-5, 16)
- An economic capital (Rev. 18)
- A political capital (Rev. 17:9-15)

Traditionally, expositors have tried to peg each of these symbols to a single entity. For example, many commentators insist the Whore of Babylon stands for the Vatican—and only the Vatican. Others believe that the Beast refers to the final kingdom—and nothing but the final kingdom.

However, such rigid interpretations inevitably fail once the remaining details of the prophecy are applied. (For example, one look at Revelation 18 tells us the Whore of Babylon, in addition to being a religious capital, also serves as the capital of a global economic empire.) Therefore, interpreting the symbols on a "single-entity" basis is a faulty method of interpretation because it produces a slew of contradictions and disagreements.

On the other hand, if we simply acknowledge that, in the book of Revelation, each symbol or "creature" has two or three different aspects, and allow the context to tell us *which* aspect is being discussed, then all the "contradictions" surrounding the identification of these symbols are instantly resolved. Our interpretations suddenly become logical and consistent.[26]

10. The Bible uses the following imagery to symbolize kings, kingdoms, wicked cities, and Satan. It might thus be helpful to keep these icons in mind as one goes through the relevant prophecies:

o   **Beast** – A godless king, his kingdom, or Satan
    [Gen. 3:1; Is. 27:1; Dan. 7:3-26; Rev. 12:3, 13:1, 11]

o   **Horn** – An evil king, the military power of that king, or the nation(s) he commands
    [Ezek. 29:21; Dan. 7:24, 8:20; Rev. 17:12]

o   **Harlot** – A city or nation drenched in false religion
    [Jer. 3:6; Is. 1:21; Nahum 3:4; Is. 23:15; Rev. 17:5]

---

[26] The 3-in-1 concept is not foreign to Scripture. For example, the Bible clearly teaches there is only one God, but when the word "God" appears in a passage, that passage could be speaking about God the Father (e.g., Is. 63:16; Mt. 3:17), God the Holy Spirit (e.g., Ex. 35:31; Lk. 3:22), or God the Son (e.g., Pr. 2:12, Jn. 20:28). Context determines which one is in view. Similarly, the Apocalypse often uses one symbol to represent three closely related entities or aspects thereof. Our job is to determine which entity or aspect is in view, based on the context and a bit of common sense.

○ **Tree:**

    – Israel
      [Mt. 24:32 (the "fig tree"); Judges 9:7-15 ("the
      trees"); Mk. 11:13, 20 (the "fig tree"); 2 Kings 19:23
      (the "tall cedar trees")]

    – The Gentile nations
      [Lk. 21:29 ("all the trees"); Rom. 11:16-27 (the
      "branches")]

    – Christ
      [Jer. 17:8; Job 14:7; Ps. 52:8; Hos. 14:5-8; Is. 11:1]

    – Antichrist Type
      [Dan. 4:10-12 (Nebuchadnezzar); Judges 9:14-15
      (Abimelech); Ezek. 31:3-14 (Asnapper the
      "Assyrian")]

APPENDIX B

ADDITIONAL EVIDENCE THAT "REVEALED" MEANS *UNLEASHED* — NOT *IDENTIFIED*

In the interest of leaving no stone unturned when it comes to Second Thessalonians, I have provided some additional evidence regarding the meaning of the word "revealed" in that book. This includes the testimony of experts, the established nature of languages, and some plain old-fashioned logic:

1. TACIT ADMISSION BY PROPHECY EXPERTS

To begin with, many well-known prophecy experts actually *agree* with the idea that the word "revealed" in Second Thessalonians 2:6 and 2:8 means to be "unleashed" or to "come to power."

We know they agree because they have taken these *same verses* and used them to prove that the Antichrist cannot "come to power" until after the Rapture:

Ron Rhodes – "This removal of the Holy Spirit's restraint allows the antichrist…to <u>come into power</u> during the tribulation period."[27]

Tim Gibson – "The Antichrist <u>cannot come to power</u> until the church's restraining influence is removed (2 Thess. 2:6-7)."[28]

Andy Woods – "Antichrist <u>cannot come to power</u> until the restrainer is removed."[29]

---

[27] *Unmasking the Antichrist*, by Ron Rhodes (Harvest House, 2012), p. 100.

[28] https://aplaceforyou.org/pastor-blog/does-the-bible-teach-a-rapture/

[29] https://www.deanbibleministries.org/dbmfiles/slides/2016-EschatologySeminar-Woods-001.pdf

John MacArthur – "Until the Holy Spirit gets out of the way, the Antichrist cannot come."[30]

Ed Hindson – "This secular Antichrist from the former Roman Empire will come to power after the rapture."[31]

Mark Hitchcock – "The rapture will throw the door wide open for the Antichrist to come to power and bring forth an outbreak of evil unlike anything that has ever occurred before."[32]

Daymond Duck – "I believe he [the Antichrist] rises to power after the Rapture of the Church."[33]

John Hagee – "The Antichrist will come to power right after the Church of Jesus Christ leaves this earth [at the Rapture]."[34]

To be sure, these good men would undoubtedly say the primary meaning of Second Thessalonians 2:6 and 2:8 is that the Antichrist cannot be "identified" today. But these eight examples confirm that they also acknowledge (unwittingly, perhaps) that the word *apokalupto* means to be *unleashed,* or to *come and take power.* They themselves have said it.

Needless to say, I agree with the experts on that.

But there's more…

---

[30] *Antichrist Unleashed,* by John MacArthur. Please see https://www.gty.org/library/sermons-library/81-47/antichrist-unleashed

[31] *15 Future Events That Will Shake the World,* by Ed Hindson (Harvest House; 2014).

[32] *Who Is the Antichrist?* by Mark Hitchcock (Harvest House, 2011), p. 38.

[33] https://christinprophecyblog.org/2009/06/could-antichrist-be-alive-today/

[34] Twitter - 9/2/2016

2. TACIT ADMISSION FROM BIBLE SCHOLARS

In addition to the aforementioned prophecy experts, many *Bible scholars* also admit that the word *apokalupto* in 2 Thessalonians means to "come to power" or to "emerge as a world leader."

This is evident from the way they translate verse 2:6 in their Bibles:

> **CEV** – You already know what is holding this wicked one back until it is time for him **to come**.

> **PHILLIPS** – I expect you remember now how I talked about this when I was with you. You will probably also remember how I used to talk about a "restraining power" which would operate until the time should come for **the emergence** of this man.

> **TLB** – And you know what is keeping him from being here already; for **he can come** only when his time is ready.

Clearly, these quotations prove that at least some scholars believe that "revealed" should be translated as "to come" or "to emerge" in Second Thessalonians. In other words, they agree with my premise.

I'll grant that their Bibles are not word-for-word translations. Instead, they are concept-for-concept. But that is precisely the point. These scholars easily could've rendered the pertinent verses to say the Antichrist won't be **identified** until the Restrainer is removed at the Rapture. But they didn't do that. Instead, realizing that the concept being conveyed is that the Antichrist cannot *come to power* until after the Church is gone, they translated these verses as saying that, once the Rapture takes place, then the restrainer will **stop holding back** the Antichrist and, instead, allow him to **emerge** and **come** forward.[35]

And that explains why...

---

[35] The word *apokalupto* has even more connotations than those above. According to scholars, it can also be translated as "breaking through" (Rom. 1:18, The Voice Bible), "erupt" (Rom. 1:18, The Message Bible), or even "come again" (Lk. 17:30, ERV, EXB, ICB, NCB).

3. NOT ONE BIBLE TRANSLATES "REVEALED" AS "IDENTIFIED"

If Second Thessalonians 2:3, 2:6, and 2:8 meant what the prophecy experts claim—namely, that the Antichrist cannot be *identified* until after the Rapture—then we would expect at least one Bible version to render the word "revealed" as *named* or *identified*.

Yet, not one Bible of any kind translates the word "revealed" as "named" or "identified." *Not one.* That is a glaring inconsistency. And it's significant, because it undermines the entire argument that we cannot know the identity of the Antichrist today. In fact, without a mis-reading of Second Thessalonians, which is (unfortunately) so common today, there is no direct evidence for the idea that the Antichrist cannot be discovered at the present time. None whatsoever.

And that is precisely why the experts have been forced to alter God's Word on the matter...

4. BAD THEOLOGY ULTIMATELY REQUIRES CHANGING GOD'S WORD

Although prophecy experts and scholars deserve our highest esteem and respect, it seems that by embracing the doctrine of *"The Church cannot know who the Antichrist is,"* they have painted themselves into a corner. Why? Because once they accept this point of view, they are forced to stretch the words of Scripture, or outright change them, in order to make everything fit.

In evidence, allow me to present several bits of *conventional wisdom* which are often invoked by the experts to make their case—yet which go directly against the Word of God:

- Speaking about who is meant to decipher the 666 code, John wrote to the **Churches** and commanded **them**: "Let him that hath understanding count the number of the beast: for it is the number of a man; and his number is Six hundred threescore and six." (Rev. 13:18).

Yet many prophecy experts have *changed* that to, "Let some **post-Rapture believer** who will be engulfed in the Tribulation count the number of the beast," even though breaking the 666 code at that time won't serve any meaningful purpose, and despite the fact that every Christian at that point will be busy evading the authorities and fighting for his very survival —not trying to break biblical codes.

- Speaking about the imminent Rapture, Jesus said, "But of that **day and hour** knoweth no man" (Mt. 24:36).

  But conventional wisdom has *extrapolated* that statement to, "But of the **Antichrist's identity** knoweth no man," because (presumably) if we did know the Antichrist's identity, then we'd have a 'not later than' date for the Rapture—about 80 years after his birth—and that would destroy imminence, even though we *already know* that Jesus is due to return within one generation of 1948, and even though, after learning the Antichrist's identity, we would still have to behave as though the Rapture could happen at any moment.

- Speaking about the fact that it will be *impossible* for people to recognize the Antichrist *immediately after the Rapture*, Paul wrote, "For this reason God sends them a **powerful delusion** so that **they will believe the lie** [regarding who the Antichrist really is]" (2 Thess. 2:11).

  But conventional wisdom has *changed* that to, "Then shall everyone see right through the delusion that God has sent and instantly recognize the Son of Hell."

- Speaking about the birth of the Antichrist, John said that he saw one Dragon, one Beast, one place, one moment, just once (Rev. 13:1).

But conventional wisdom has *changed* that to, "The Dragon has been roaming all over the earth for two thousand years, continually vetting and grooming dozens of Antichrist hopefuls as they rise and fall on the stage of history, because not even Satan can know who the Antichrist is."

So much for conventional wisdom.

The direct and repeated testimony of Scripture, on the other hand, is that we *can know* the identity of the Antichrist. He will rise only *once* in history.[36] And that will occur in just *one location*:

- **Revelation 13:1** (NIV) — *"The dragon stood on the shore of the sea. And I saw a beast coming out of the sea."*

  One Dragon, one Beast, one place, one moment, just once.

- **Revelation 13:18** (HCSB) — *"The one who has <u>understanding</u> must calculate the number of the beast."*

  The Church is commanded to solve the 666 code because she is the only entity that possesses the *understanding* necessary to solve these mysteries (James 1:5; 1 Cor. 12:8; Jn. 16:13; Eph. 3:10). Therefore, only the Church has the power to unscramble the 666 code. And she has been *ordered* to do so.

- **Revelation 22:7** (NKJV) — *"Behold, I am coming quickly! Blessed is he who <u>keeps the words</u> of the prophecy of this book."*

  The Church is the only entity that is told to *keep all the words of the Apocalypse.* Therefore, it is the *Church* whom God expects to solve the 666 enigma.

---

[36] That is, notwithstanding the Antichrist's initial appearance in the First Century A.D. as one of the five Roman Caesars: Augustus, Tiberius, Caligula, Claudius, or Nero. Please see *Empire of the Antichrist* (Positron Books, 2021) for more information on this topic.

- **1 John 4:1, 3** — *"Beloved, do not believe every spirit, but <u>test the spirits</u> whether they are of God...and every spirit that does not confess that Jesus Christ has come in the flesh...this is the spirit of the Antichrist, which you have heard was coming."*

  The only entity that John calls "beloved" is the *Church*. Therefore, it is the *Church* that is advised to *test* the spirits to see if any are anti-christ, and to see if one of them is *the* Antichrist whom we have heard is "coming."

- **Matthew 24:4-5** (NASB) — *"<u>See to it</u> that no one misleads you. For many will come in My name, saying, 'I am the Christ.'"*

  As followers of Jesus, we must see to it that no one misleads us into chasing false christs, and one of the best ways to do that is by knowing the career, character, and perhaps even the identity of the greatest false christ in history.

In light of all this evidence, I believe it is time for the experts to abandon their position on this matter and acknowledge that the word "revealed" in Second Thessalonians does not mean to be identified. It means to be "unleashed" or "empowered."

And we can add even more weight to this point of view by simply realizing who "owns" the riddle of the Eighth King...

5. THE CHURCH OWNS THE RIDDLE OF THE "EIGHTH KING"

In Revelation 17, one of the angels of Almighty God gives John a number of clues that can finally unlock the identity of the Beast—a.k.a., the "Eighth King"—along with the identities of his cohorts. By providing these clues to John, God is signaling that the *Church* is the one who's expected to solve this riddle and identify the Antichrist.

After all: *Why would God provide John with so much "classified" information, say that the solution requires godly "wisdom," and then command the apostle to send this data to the Church, if God did not expect the* Church *to figure out the identities of these strange beings*:

THE RIDDLE

Revelation 17:7-12, 18 — And the angel said unto me, Wherefore didst thou marvel? I will tell **thee** [John, and by implication his audience, the Church] the mystery of the woman, and of the **beast** that carrieth her, which hath the seven heads and ten horns.

The **beast** that thou sawest was, and is not; and shall ascend out of the bottomless pit, and go into perdition: and they that dwell on the earth shall wonder, whose names were not written in the book of life from the foundation of the world, when they behold the beast that was, and is not, and yet is.

And here is the mind which hath **wisdom**. The seven **heads** are seven **mountains** [hills], on which the woman sitteth. And there are seven **kings**: five are fallen, and one is, and the other is not yet come; and when he cometh, he must continue a short space.

And the **beast** that was, and is not, even **he is the eighth** [**king**], and is of the seven, and goeth into perdition.

And the ten **horns** which thou sawest are ten **kings**, which have received no kingdom as yet; but receive power as kings one hour with the beast...

And the **woman** which thou sawest is that great **city**, which reigneth over the kings of the earth.

THE IMPLIED OWNER

Revelation 1:1 — The Revelation of Jesus Christ, which God gave unto him, **to shew unto his servants**...

Revelation 1:4 — John **to the seven churches** which are in Asia.

> Note – By addressing his letter to "the seven churches" in verse 4 above, John is equating the *churches*, not post-Rapture saints, with the term "his servants," which appears right before this in verse 1.

Revelation 22:6 — And he said unto me, These sayings are faithful and true: and the Lord God of the holy prophets sent his angel to shew **unto his servants** [i.e., **the churches**] the things which must shortly be done.

Revelation 22:10 — And he saith unto me, **Seal not the sayings of the prophecy of this book**: for the time is at hand.

Revelation 22:12 — And, behold, **I come quickly**; and my reward is with me...

Revelation 22:16 — I Jesus have sent mine angel to testify unto you these things **in the churches**.

The logical conclusion demanded by these verses is inescapable: God expects the identity of the Antichrist, or **"Eighth King"** to be deciphered by his servants—the members of the Church—before Jesus "comes quickly" at the Rapture. They are the ones who "own" this riddle. They are the ones who have the godly "wisdom" needed to decipher it. They are the ones *explicitly* to whom this message has been sent.

Post-Rapture saints, on the other hand, do not have the "wisdom" to solve this riddle, nor is it even addressed to them. In fact, by definition, they won't even consider these passages until *after* Jesus "comes quickly." They are nowhere in the picture. So why put them there?

6. SCRIPTURE CANNOT GO AGAINST SCRIPTURE

Next on the list of proofs is a *basic truth* that every Christian should know: God does not make contradictory statements. Not ever (Nu. 23:19). And that axiom is especially critical to this discussion because the Holy Spirit actually *commanded* the Church to identify the Antichrist:

> **1 John 4:1, 3** — Beloved, do not believe every spirit, but **test the spirits** …[including]… the spirit of the Antichrist, which you have heard was coming.

> **Matthew 24:4-5** (NASB) — **See to it** that **no one misleads you**. For many will come in My name, saying, 'I am the Christ.'

> **Revelation 13:18** (HCSB) — The one who has understanding **must calculate** the number of the beast, because it is the number of a man. His number is 666.

> **Revelation 22:10, 22:7** — **Seal not** the sayings of the prophecy of this book: for the time is at hand…. [B]lessed is he that **keepeth** the sayings of the prophecy of this book.

Notice that each of these statements is a command. And all of them are interrelated. God has ordered us to: 1) *calculate* the number of the Beast, 2) *seal not* the words of the Apocalypse, 3) *keep all the words* of the Apocalypse, including the 666 code, 4) *test* the spirits to see if any are anti-christ, or perhaps even *the* Antichrist, and 5) *make sure* that no "false christ" misleads us, especially the greatest false christ in history.

It is therefore impossible for the Holy Spirit to have *countermanded* these orders elsewhere in Scripture. That is, he would not have told us to stay alert for false Christs and to use the 666 code to identify the ultimate Antichrist, and then turned around and said, *Don't even try to find the Antichrist!*

That would be a blatant contradiction in God's Word—and we know that, for God, that just isn't possible (1 Cor. 14:33; Pr. 30:5; Heb. 6:17-18; James 1:17, etc.)

7. LANGUAGES CHANGE OVER TIME

As most people know, languages change over time. And Old English is no exception. Just consider the following examples:

WORD	OLD ENGLISH MEANING	MODERN ENGLISH MEANING
Let	Restrain or hold back	Allow or permit
Conversation	Lifestyle	Discussion
Naughty	Poor	Immoral
Nice	Naive or gullible	Pleasant
Dinner	Breakfast	Supper
Awful	Awe-inspiring	Repulsive
Suffer	Allow or permit	Endure pain
Mean	Inferior	Cruel

Likewise, even though "revealed" now means to uncover, unveil, or identify, in 1611 A.D., when the King James Version was published, that word *also* meant "to come to power," or "to be unleashed." [37]

Consequently (etymologically speaking), the idea that Paul is telling us the Antichrist will be unleashed and come to power following the Rapture—*not that he will suddenly be identifiable*—is on very solid ground.

8. THE CHURCH WOULD BLOW THE WHISTLE ON THE GUY

A popular prophecy expert recently claimed that it is absolutely impossible for the Church to ID the Antichrist because, if we did, we would "blow the whistle on the guy." The expert's implication was that if the Church actually spotted the Antichrist, it would have him arrested and the Tribulation would be completely averted.

---

[37] For example, when Paul says in Romans 1:18, "For the wrath of God is **revealed** from heaven," we understand that he means, *For the wrath of God is **unleashed** from heaven.*

Again, when Paul says in 2 Thessalonians 1:7-8, "[T]he Lord Jesus shall be **revealed** from heaven…taking vengeance on those who do not know God," we understand that he means, *The Lord Jesus will **burst** out of heaven and **unleash** his vengeance on the ungodly.*

Even today, in almost every language, a given word often has more than one meaning. This is what allows people to write poetry, use hyperbole, make a pun, or employ a double entendre. For example, notice how many ways the word "run" is used in the following sentences:

> I came home one day and announced I was *running* for office. Naturally, the kids got excited and started *running* around the house. But they soon *ran* out of energy. So, my wife *ran* to the store to get some snacks. That's when she noticed a *run* in her stockings. But the store had *run up* the price for nylons. So, she *ran down* the manager and asked for a discount. But the manager said that all sales had finished their *runs*. So, by the time my wife got back to the house, she felt very *run-down*.

Clearly, the word "run" does not always mean to sprint or to jog. There are many variations, based on usage and context. It should therefore come as no surprise that the word "revealed" in 2 Thessalonians can also mean something other than "identified."

A few simple questions show why this line of reasoning is nonsense:

- To whom, exactly, would the Church report this discovery?

- Would any government agency actually pay attention to this?

- What action would the Church demand the authorities take (besides an arrest), and what would be the legal justification for demanding such action?

- Would "blowing the whistle on the guy" stop the Antichrist from carrying out any of the prophecies that have already been recorded in Scripture? Would it stop Armageddon or the return of Jesus?

Let's be level-headed about this. If God did reveal the Antichrist to the Church, it would not be so that we could "blow the whistle on the guy." It would not be so that we could report him to the FBI, the CIA, Interpol, or any other secular authority. Nor would it be so that we could take matters into our own hands. Instead, it would be to motivate us to stay pure — and to evangelize others — as we wait for the Rapture, because if we *did* spot the Antichrist, we would see the day is approaching, and we would know for certain that time is short.

CONCLUSION

Given all of this evidence, not to mention the evidence that was presented in Chapter 3 of this book, it should now be abundantly clear that the word "revealed" in 2 Thessalonians is not being used to say the Antichrist can only be "identified" after the Rapture. It is being used to say he will suddenly be "unleashed" once the restraining influence of the Holy Spirit (through the Church) is removed.

Indeed, as a direct result of the Antichrist's being unleashed—not *identified*—Jesus will come and destroy him with the Shekinah glory of God (2 Thess. 2:8).

And thus, our initial argument is now stronger than ever: Neither Paul's second letter to the Thessalonians, nor anything else in the Bible, prevents the Church from identifying the Antichrist today.

APPENDIX C

2 THESSALONIANS 2:1-8 (paraphrased)

Words in boldface indicate text which has been replaced to match my understanding of the passage. This is not a translation of the original manuscript or an alteration of God's Word. It is simply my paraphrase:

> [1] Now we **plead with you, brothers, about** the coming of our Lord Jesus Christ **at the Rapture,** [2] **Please do not be** shaken in mind, or troubled, neither by spirit, nor by word, nor by letter as from us, **stating** that the **Tribulation has already started.**
>
> [3] Let no man deceive you by any means: for the **Tribulation shall not start,** except there come **the Rapture** first, and that man of sin **come to power,** the son of perdition; [4] Who opposeth and exalteth himself above all that is called God, or that is worshipped; so that he as God sitteth in the temple of God, shewing himself that he is God.
>
> [5] Remember ye not, that, when I was yet with you, I told you these things. [6] And now **you know what is holding the Antichrist back until it is time for him to be unleashed.** [7] **Because even though the forces of Satan are hard at work, the One who now holds back the Antichrist will continue to hold him back,** until **that same One is** taken out of the way. [8] And then shall **the Antichrist be let loose,** whom the Lord shall consume with the spirit of his mouth, and shall destroy with the brightness of his coming.

In essence, Paul is telling the Thessalonians they can relax because: first, the Church will be raptured, then the Holy Spirit will stop restraining the forces of Satan, and *then* the Antichrist will be unleashed to do his evil deeds. Hence, Paul is calming the Thessalonians by saying they will be raptured before the Antichrist *comes to power*, not before he's *identified*. And that means Second Thessalonians does not rule out the possibility the Antichrist will be identified today, nor does it prohibit the Church from looking for that monster right now.

ADDITIONAL POSITRON BOOKS

God Says Count the Number 666! Why the Church Can Discover the Identity of the Antichrist! (2022)

- Has Satan been grooming an Antichrist candidate in each generation?
- Is the 666 code meant for post-Rapture believers...or the Church?
- How does God use prophecy to save people from judgment?
- Does "imminence" prevent the Church from discovering the Beast?
- Which verse says the Antichrist cannot be identified till after the Rapture? (Hint: There is none!)

Empire of the Antichrist (2020)

- Where is the first prophecy recorded in Scripture?
- Which empire of history is the last empire of prophecy?
- Who are the Beast, the Seven Heads, and the Ten Horns?
- Who—or what—is the Whore of Babylon?
- Will the Antichrist be American, Arab, Persian, or Roman?
- Which verse controls the order and content of Daniel and Revelation?

The Islamic Antichrist Myth (2020)

- Where is "Satan's throne" located
- How can an Islamic leader claim to be God?
- Will Muslims actually worship the Antichrist?
- Will the Antichrist conquer all the previous empires of prophecy?
- Is the Beast of Revelation an Arab, a Persian, a Turk...or an Italian?

Coming soon...

The Whore of Babylon (2024)

- Is she a country, a religion, an economic empire...or an ancient city?
- Why was John scolded for being "amazed" at her appearance?
- What does her title "Babylon the Great" really mean?
- Why will the Antichrist and his cohorts destroy her?
- How can she "sit" on the Beast?

Gog of Magog (2025)

- Is Gog a Russian strongman...or the Roman Antichrist?
- Will Gog's War take place when the Tribulation begins...or ends?
- Is Gog's War really just another name for Armageddon?
- Can we construct a Tribulation timeline, based on Scripture?
- Is the Whore of Babylon punished once...or twice?

The False Prophet (2025)

- Is the False Prophet a Jew or a Gentile?
- Was he born before, during, or after 1948?
- Why does the False Prophet have two horns like a lamb?
- Is the False Prophet admired and respected by Christians today?
- What does the Bible mean when it says he will "speak like a dragon"?

The Antichrist (2025)

- Where will the Antichrist come from? Is he alive today?
- Is he a master of the occult? What does the 666 code mean?
- Is he a homosexual...or is he married with children?
- Is he a Secular Humanist, a Jew, or a Muslim?
- Is he the biological offspring of Satan?

What Every Christian Should Know (2025)

Believe it or not, a recent survey shows that most Christians have trouble correctly defining the Gospel. Many are unable to properly state what it takes for a person to be saved. And only a handful can list the Ten Commandments. So imagine having a small pamphlet that can boost one's knowledge of Christian fundamentals, and provide the necessary foundation upon which to lead others to Christ. Brief and to the point, this book clears up many misconceptions and enables believers to "know what they believe." Great for new Christians!

How to Witness Like Jesus and the Apostles (2025)

Would you be surprised to learn that Jesus *never* said:

- You should thoroughly befriend people before witnessing to them.
- There's a God-shaped hole in your heart that only the Lord can fill.
- God has a wonderful plan for your life.
- God is not angry with sinners.

Learn how Jesus *actually* presented the Gospel to others. No one did it better!

Darwin's Apocalypse (2025)

- Why do so many biologists privately admit that Evolution is false?
- How many laws of nature does the theory of Evolution violate?
- Do programs like AVIDA prove Evolution is true...or just the opposite?
- Has anyone ever seen Evolution produce a new kind of animal?
- Why is the following equation fatally flawed:

$$(\text{Random Mutation} \times \text{Natural Selection})^n = \text{New Species}$$

Please visit Prophecy7000.com for updates!

ABOUT THE AUTHOR

Charles "Ken" Bassett has enjoyed the study of prophecy ever since a friend handed him a copy of Hal Lindsey's *The Late, Great Planet Earth* in 1978. Shortly after that pivotal moment, Charles gave his life to Christ and began searching the Scriptures to see what God says about such topics as the Rapture, the Tribulation, the Antichrist, and the glorious return of Jesus.

Realizing that a wealth of end-time information and insight also exists in the writings of incredibly gifted scholars, pastors, and expositors, Charles began devouring their works, as well.

Now, after a lifetime of study, Charles has put forth his own observations on such topics as the Beast, the False Prophet, and the Whore of Babylon. However, he says, the belief that no one can discover the identity of the Antichrist until after the Rapture is not taught in Scripture. Instead, not only does the Bible permit such a discovery, but both Jesus and John said the Church should make an attempt to identify the Beast and break the 666 code.

On a more personal note, Charles now lives near Austin, Texas, with his college sweetheart and wife of forty-five years, Denise. They have five grown children and seven grandchildren. During the 1980s, Charles was a T-37 instructor pilot and a C-141 airlift pilot with the United States Air Force. Afterwards, he was hired by a major airline, where he was employed for 36 years and enjoyed flying international routes as a B-777 captain.

In addition to *God Says Count the Number 666!* and other related titles, Charles has also published a children's book, *Timmy and His Flying Saucer*, through Christian Faith Publishing.

Email: ckbassett777@yahoo.com

www.ingramcontent.com/pod-product-compliance
Lightning Source LLC
Chambersburg PA
CBHW051835040426
42447CB00006B/538